Opportunity from Strength:
Strategic Planning Clarified with Case Examples

by Robert G. Cope

ASHE-ERIC Higher Education Report No. 8, 1987

Prepared by

Clearinghouse on Higher Education
The George Washington University

Published by

Association for the Study of
Higher Education

Jonathan D. Fife,
Series Editor

Cite as
Cope, Robert G. *Opportunity from Strength: Strategic Planning Clarified with Case Examples.* ASHE-ERIC Higher Education Report No. 8. Washington, D.C.: Association for the Study of Higher Education, 1987.

Managing Editor: Christopher Rigaux
Manuscript Editor: Barbara M. Fishel/Editech

The ERIC Clearinghouse on Higher Education invites individuals to submit proposals for writing monographs for the Higher Education Report series. Proposals must include:
1. A detailed manuscript proposal of not more than five pages.
2. A chapter-by-chapter outline.
3. A 75-word summary to be used by several review committees for the initial screening and rating of each proposal.
4. A vita.
5. A writing sample.

Library of Congress Catalog Card Number 88-71518
ISSN 0884-0040
ISBN 0-913317-43–8

Cover design by Michael David Brown, Rockville, Maryland

ERIC **Clearinghouse on Higher Education**
School of Education and Human Development
The George Washington University
One Dupont Circle, Suite 630
Washington, D.C. 20036-1183

ASHE Association for the Study of Higher Education
Texas A&M University
Department of Educational Administration
Harrington Education Center
College Station, Texas 77843

This publication was prepared partially with funding from the Office of Educational Research and Improvement, U.S. Department of Education, under contract no. 400-86-0017. The opinions expressed in this report do not necessarily reflect the positions or policies of OERI or the Department.

EXECUTIVE SUMMARY

The term "strategic" usually associated with "planning" has been applied to virtually every administrative action in higher education over the past six or so years. The term has been overused and frequently incorrectly applied. This report identifies appropriate and inappropriate uses of the concept, reviews the significant literature that provides both conceptual and practical guidelines, presents a series of very simple to more complex planning models institutions can adopt or modify, depending upon their circumstances, to plan strategically, and illustrates the use of various strategic planning models with case examples.

What Are the Major Mistakes Made in Strategic Planning?
The strategic concept for direction finding should limit it to decisions associated with positioning in the external environment so that the acquisition of resources is enhanced. The strategy concept for managing limits its use to decisions associated with the implementation of strategies and the efficient use of resources. One important distinction—seldom made—is to separate the "where" from the "how." Where to go is strategizing; how to accomplish the strategy is management—or quite simply, planning. Strategizing takes place when an institution does not have control in its external environment if opportunities and threats occur. Management is appropriate when an institution does have control over its own resources, structures, personnel, information systems, and so on. Most strategic analyses do not make that important distinction, and the results of planning are then—as new research has shown—less beneficial.

With leadership appropriate to the strategic concept, an institution will develop a widespread capability among staff to think strategically and will seek to develop a strategic framework from which it will compete for resources in future environments. Thus, leadership provides an institution with a continuing capacity to plan strategically that, for that institution, results in a strategic framework, not just plans.

**Are Some Foundations and Fundamentals
Not Well Understood?**
Although strategic planning is widely assumed to have started in the business community in the 1960s and in higher education in the early 1980s, the foundations of the strategic concept can be traced to at least 500 B.C. Its conceptual origins are deeply imbedded in the geopolitical and biological disciplines. Because

of the resulting richness of the concept, it has been linked to many other concepts of organization; however, not all organizations are equally able to apply the concept. The application of the concept depends upon the degree to which an institution has control over price (tuition, overhead charges), range of products (programs and degrees), and location (where it offers services and attracts resources).

Positioning occurs on both macro and micro levels. The institution seeks a direction of travel in the macro environment; its departments have micro positions to occupy. Their strategic positioning together results in a *strategic framework* that allows them to compete for resources in future environments.

Do Institutions Waste Resources Doing Too Much Environmental Scanning and Gathering Too Much Information?

The key to planning strategically is simple environmental scanning. Institutions regularly assess changes occurring in their environments at two levels: institution and department. The institution assesses megatrends; departments assess trends in their discipline/profession. Most scanning is passive; most of the information needed to make strategic choices is already in the minds of the participants. As the cases illustrate, most strategizing can be done much faster and with much less expense.

The report identifies faculty, trustees, and administrators as already highly informed processors of qualitative information needing little of what most management information systems provide to make strategic choices. Management information systems are, however, important for control and for determining progress toward achievement of plans.

The report illustrates relatively simple, low-cost, and fast-working models for both environmental scanning and information collection. It is central to the effectiveness of the strategy concept that it be driven by ideas, not by data and paper. An important result of a strategic planning process is to develop a widespread approach to thinking strategically, what Bennis and Nanus (1985) call "organizational learning."

The report also includes 11 case examples to illustrate appropriate and inappropriate applications of the strategic concept. The cases demonstrate a wide variety of strategic planning approaches that depend always on the circumstances of that institution at that time. The University of Minnesota and Carnegie-Mellon University are shown to follow—with quite different results—clear presidential leadership models to get the institutions started. Carnegie-Mellon University also illustrates developing strategic frameworks. Millikin University demonstrates that strategic planning does not necessarily result in organizational change when it is determined that a satisfactory strategic framework is already in place. Center-Right University illustrates the competitive purposes, sometimes secretive applications, of strategic thinking and illustrates how planning should take place in at least two organizational levels. The strategic planning at Iowa State University, Edmonds Community College, and the College of Education at San Diego State University illustrates the use of a simple model of strategic planning, while the case example from Caring Arts College illustrates a longer, structured process. Another process, involving a third party, is illustrated by the case of the Southwest Joint Center for Education. Bradley University illustrates the use of the strategic concept for both academic and nonacademic program review. And the case of the "hypothetical" college of home economics illustrates most of the ideas associated with an appropriate application of the strategic concept.

Is Help Available for Both Administrators And Students of Management?

The first half of the report, written largely for the administrator, clarifies appropriate and inappropriate uses of the strategic concept, emphasizing case examples. The second portion of the report, written for the serious student of the strategic concept, relies more heavily on reviews of the literature and an analysis of techniques before becoming more theoretical.

ADVISORY BOARD

Roger G. Baldwin
Assistant Professor of Education
College of William and Mary

Carol M. Boyer
Senior Policy Analyst for Higher Education
Education Commission of the States

Clifton F. Conrad
Professor of Higher Education
Department of Educational Administration
University of Wisconsin–Madison

Elaine H. El-Khawas
Vice President
Policy Analysis and Research
American Council on Education

Martin Finkelstein
Associate Professor of Higher Education Administration
Seton Hall University

Carol Everly Floyd
Associate Vice Chancellor for Academic Affairs
Board of Regents of the Regency Universities System
State of Illinois

George D. Kuh
Associate Dean for Academic Affairs
School of Education
Indiana University

Yvonna S. Lincoln
Associate Professor of Higher Education
University of Kansas

Richard F. Wilson
Associate Chancellor
University of Illinois

Ami Zusman
Principal Analyst, Academic Affairs
University of California

CONSULTING EDITORS

Trudy W. Banta
Research Professor
University of Tennessee

Harriet W. Cabell
Associate Dean for Adult Education
Director, External Degree Program
University of Alabama

L. Leon Campbell
Provost and Vice President for Academic Affairs
University of Delaware

Ellen Earle Chaffee
Associate Commissioner for Academic Affairs
North Dakota State Board of Higher Education

Peter T. Ewell
Senior Associate
National Center for Higher Education Management Systems

Reynolds Ferrante
Professor of Higher Education
George Washington University

J. Wade Gilley
Senior Vice President
George Mason University

Judy Diane Grace
Director of Research
Council for Advancement and Support of Education

Madeleine F. Green
Director, Center for Leadership Development
American Council on Education

Milton Greenberg
Provost
American University

Judith Dozier Hackman
Associate Dean
Yale University

Paul W. Hartman
Vice Chancellor for University Relations and Development
Texas Christian University

James C. Hearn
Associate Professor
University of Minnesota

Margaret Heim
Senior Research Officer
Teachers Insurance and Annuity Association/
  College Retirement Equity Fund

Evelyn Hively
Vice President for Academic Programs
American Association of State Colleges and Universities

Frederic Jacobs
Dean of the Faculties
American University

Paul Jedamus
Professor
University of Colorado

Hans H. Jenny
Executive Vice President
Chapman College

Joseph Katz
Director, New Jersey Master Faculty Program
Woodrow Wilson National Fellowship Foundation

George Keller
Senior Vice President
The Barton-Gillet Company

L. Lee Knefelkamp
Dean, School of Education
American University

David A. Kolb
Professor and Chairman
Department of Organizational Behavior
The Weatherhead School of Management
Case Western Reserve University

Oscar T. Lenning
Executive Vice President
Dean of Academic Affairs
Waldorf College

Charles J. McClain
President
Northeast Missouri State University

Judith B. McLaughlin
Research Associate on Education and Sociology
Harvard University

James L. Morrison
Professor
University of North Carolina

Sheila A. Murdick
Director, National Program on Noncollegiate-Sponsored
  Instruction
New York State Board of Regents

Elizabeth M. Nuss
Executive Director
National Association of Student Personnel Administrators

Steven G. Olswang
Assistant Provost for Academic Affairs
University of Washington

Robert L. Payton
Scholar-in-Residence in Philanthropic Studies
University of Virginia

Henry A. Spille
Director, Office on Educational Credits and Credentials
American Council on Education

CONTENTS

TABLES AND FIGURES

Tables

Figures

FOREWORD

Strategic planning has been an increasingly popular concept within higher education policy circles for almost a decade. To some institutions this particular planning process has achieved its promise, but for many others it has been less than successful. An underlying issue is to identify why strategic planning has not worked or to put it in a better light, how strategic planning has been effective.

As Robert Cope clearly emphasizes in this report, the unique characteristic of strategic planning is an acknowledgement that uncontrollable external influences play a large part in charting an institution's course and therefore it is necessary to use environmental scanning as a central process to assess the potential impact of these forces.[1] While this point is a central theme of this report, Cope's main purpose is to present specific case study examples that clearly demonstrate why and how strategic planning has succeeded or failed, and how an institution regardless of its size can benefit from the correct use of strategic planning.

Strategic planning must become an organizational goal to be successful, according to Bob Cope, associate professor of higher education at the University of Washington and author of the now sold-out AAHE-ERIC monograph, *Strategic Planning, Management, and Decision Making*. Like any management tool, its effectiveness is determined by the skill of the personnel implementing it. And since organizational planning is not a solitary activity, it is necessary to have much of the institutional leadership at the same skill level. This report, widely shared, will help ensure greater effectiveness in institutional planning.

Jonathan D. Fife
Professor and Director
ERIC Clearinghouse on Higher Education
School of Education and Human Development
The George Washington University

---

[1]This methodology as well as future research techniques have been addressed in a previous monograph, *Futures Research and the Strategic Planning Process: Implications for Higher Education* by James Morrison, William Renfro, and Wayne Boucher, released as Report 9, 1984.

ACKNOWLEDGMENTS

The reader of this report will benefit greatly from the valued contributions of five anonymous reviewers. I am particularly grateful for the ideas shared over the years by Nancy Borton, Ellen Chaffee, Warren Groff, Judith Hackman, Richard Ireland, George Keller, Oscar Lenning, Mark Meredith, Ann Morey, James Morrison, and Marvin Peterson, whether reviewers or not. Dwight Paulson suggested the title and many trusting administrators allowed me on their campuses. The national debt is burnt peanuts compared with mine.

Robert Cope
Seattle, Washington

CLARIFYING STRATEGIC PLANNING

Strategic planning visibly started with George Keller's *Academic Strategy* in 1983, one of the largest-selling books ever written on the management of the academy. Its subsequent widespread use suggests that, where properly conceived and carried out, the application of the strategic concept leads to improved institutional vitality, which—in this report—is defined as a combination of success and prosperity: *Success* in mission fulfillment with the acquisition of sufficient resources for *prosperity.*

Written mostly for the benefit of the practitioner, this report seeks to clarify, to illustrate, and to provide some understanding of the depth of this concept by:

- Introducing a model recommended for further research and practice in an effort to clarify strategic planning;
- Using case examples to illustrate both good and less effective practices; and
- Focusing on additional variations of the topic to contribute to a greater depth of understanding and resulting skills in application.

Strategic planning appears to have one essential characteristic: It is direction finding for the whole enterprise in relation to the ecosystem.

While the report begins with clarification and cases, it then purposely weaves concepts, practices, models, and case examples into each other throughout the remainder of the report because that is fundamental to the concept itself: It is layered and multidimensional, drawing on many disciplines and largely mirroring the complexity of people, institutions, and environments in living interaction. The report also includes a section on theory.

Why Strategic Planning?
The strategic concept is at once simple and complex. Part of the concept's popularity is no doubt because of its rich intellectual challenge and its range of applications in practice. The strategic concept moves an organization's attention to higher-than-usual levels of complexity: not just organization, but organization and environment; not just now, but then, now, and someday; not just data, but wisdom; not just participation, but consensus building.

The higher education community appears to have grasped strategic planning in the early 1980s as it attempted to respond to certain pervasive problems:

1. The institution seemed to have no clear vision of its mis-

sion, no mission, or—at best—an unclear mission. Communication throughout the institution about purpose, goals, and vision was unclear. Control was lacking.

2. The environment was quite turbulent: High school enrollments were decreasing, government policy was not predictable, new technologies (computer, biogenetics) were appearing, competing colleges were adopting new techniques of marketing.

3. Too much attention was given to short-term, internally focused problems and issues; the focus was on details, on seeing only the parts and not the whole.

4. Too much of institutions' performance was largely based on "bottom line" standards—test scores, the number of students, the size of the endowment, and so on.

5. Little connection existed between the campus master plan, the enrollment plan, and the budget plan (Freed 1987).

While such problems are good reasons for adopting the strategic concept, the primary motivators appear to have been strategic planning as a way to respond to the downturn in high school graduations and to the financial squeeze of the late 1970s and early 1980s. By the mid-1980s, strategic planning dominated both scholarly literature and the literature oriented toward practitioners (Miller 1983; Schmidtlein 1985).

In 1985, only 24 institutions in a representative sample of 196 postsecondary institutions said they were not using strategic planning (Meredith 1985). A followup study of those same institutions concluded that most of the institutions had started strategic planning to find direction, set priorities, focus effort, and in general gain more control over the institution's future (Meredith, Lenning, and Cope 1988).

What Is Strategic Planning?
Writers have struggled for some time to define strategic planning (Cope 1978, 1981, 1985a, 1985b, 1988; Freed 1987; McCune 1986; Peterson 1980; Steiner 1979b), contrasting strategic planning with other forms of planning and concluding that it is different and that the strategic concept appears to suggest the need for yet newer conceptions of management practice and theory.

The term has many definitions. From its earliest use in business to the more recent one in higher education, all relate to a management function designed to achieve goals in dynamic, competitive environments through the allocation of resources (Ansoff 1965; Chaffee and Tierney 1988; Cope 1978, 1981, 1988; Keller 1983; Peterson 1980; Peterson et al. 1986).

Most definitions say strategic planning is planning for the whole organization in reference to the organization's external environment. Proponents argue that this emphasis of whole organization to whole environment is essential to institutional vitality, even survival. Strategic planning appears to have one essential characteristic: It is direction finding for the whole enterprise in relation to the ecosystem. It is proactive.

Beyond the connection with the environment, the concept is difficult to define with precision. The usual semantic confusion exists that is true of any concept with characteristics, for example, of an academic discipline that is more art than science (Enarson 1975). The business community, with over 25 years of literature and practice with the concept, now gives little attention to definitions.

Higher education, however, still appears to need a definition for describing this form of management and for organizing research. The following definition is offered to draw attention to the essential elements of strategic planning: *Strategic planning is an open systems approach to steering an enterprise over time through uncertain environmental waters. It is a proactive problem-solving behavior directed externally at conditions in the environment and a means to find a favorable competitive position in the continual competition for resources. Its primary purpose is to achieve success with mission while linking the institution's future to anticipated changes in the environment in such a way that the acquisition of resources (money, personnel, staff, students, good will) is faster than the depletion of resources.*

This definition, because it emphasizes the acquisition of resources, gets to a key point about the "bottom-line" reason for strategic planning: prosperity. Simply put, however, strategic planning is what the enterprise does to position itself favorably relative to resources in the environment (Pfeffer and Salancik 1978; Yuchtman and Seashore 1967). Table 1 contrasts strategic planning with other forms of planning.

The distinctions made in table 1 suggest that the application of the strategic concept is on the external environment, that it is oriented toward institutional changes and directed by a vision of future states. It is oriented toward finding synergy, wholeness, effectiveness, and patterns in decision making as people

TABLE 1
DIFFERENTIATING STRATEGIC PLANNING FROM OTHER FORMS OF PLANNING

Strategic Planning	Other Planning
Emphasis on the environment	Emphasis on the enterprise
Oriented toward change	Emphasis on stability
Vision directed	Follows a blue print
Inductive and integrated	Deductive and analytical
Proactive	Reactive
Emphasis on doing the right things	Emphasis on doing things right
Art	Science
Open and external focus	Closed and internal focus
Anticipates changes	Extrapolates from the past
Current decisions based on looking from the future	Current decisions based on looking from the present
Entrepreneurial and action oriented, even when there is ambiguity	Inaction when there is ambiguity
Emphasis on innovation and creativity	Emphasis on the tried and tested
Synergistic	Univariate
Enterprise's environment and context are primary determinants of strategy/choices/direction	Enterprise's strengths and weaknesses are primary determinants of strategy/choices/direction
Emphasis on opinions, intuition, and the qualitative	Emphasis on facts and the quantitative
Orientation toward effectiveness	Orientation toward efficiency
Patterns are in a stream of decisions	Decisions are made and carried out

Source: Meredith, Cope, and Lenning 1987.

within the institution use qualitative information to inform their intuitive judgments.

Other ideas of what strategic planning means will appear in the following sections. To help organize many of those ideas, this report uses a two-part process model similar to that applied in business by one Boston consulting firm (see figure 1) (Cope 1988; Drake 1986).

The left part of the model shown in figure 1 emphasizes mission, the environment, the enterprise's strengths, and key suc-

FIGURE 1

MODEL FOR STRATEGY FORMULATION AND IMPLEMENTATION

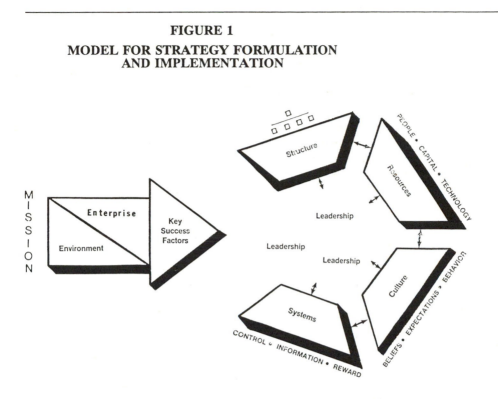

Source: Drake 1986, p. 19.

cess factors, the last of which are taken to be what an institution must do relative to its resource-providing ecosystem to be successful in fulfilling its mission with prosperity. Taken together, the key success factors contain most of the elements ascribed to a vision. For example, one of the following cases tells of an institution that purposely increased its tuition to position itself among the top one-third of institutions in its market; that institution regards the move as one of several key success factors.

As process, the left part of the model describes an intellectually demanding search that relates the institution's strengths to opportunities in the environment resulting in a future vision. According to one college president, "Strategic planning is a self-discovery process that recognizes and responds to environmental pressures and opportunities within the limits of the college's resources."* And to another, "Strategic planning is a

---

collegial process for the design of an imaginable future—one harmonizing diverse activities while providing a good fit between opportunities and strengths."*

Consistent with much of business practice that tends to encompass both strategic (left) and organizational (right) issues, *strategic plans develop from the factors on the left portion of this model.* This process is strategic formulation, taken to be direction finding relative to the environment.

The *implementation* of strategy is accomplished by changing the organizational factors to the right of the model. Implementation is shaping the enterprise, as opposed to direction finding. The arrangement of structures, the allocation of resources among competing internal demands, the development of favorable campus cultures (beliefs, expectations, and behaviors), and the application of appropriate systems (for rewards, control, and information) shape the enterprise.

This interpretation of the strategic concept as direction finding and shaping is consistent with Mintzberg's analogy of the potter with clay (1987). Strategists are craftswomen and men who have a vision of what will be and then shape the material. "The product that emerges on the wheel is likely to be in the tradition of her past work, but she may break away and embark on a new direction. Even so, the past is no less present, projecting itself into the future" (p. 66).

Nearly all of this report deals with the direction-finding, formulation dimension of the strategic concept, that is, the left side of the model.

Where Does Leadership Fit the Strategic Concept and the Model?

Leadership has been interpreted in countless ways, and it can be almost anything it is wanted to be (Stogdill 1974). For the purposes of this report—and consistent with much of the practice in higher education—it emphasizes the formulation of ideas and communication as the conceptual glues joining strategic formulation (left of the model) to implementation (right); the vision of "where" is joined through collegial leadership with application of the "how" (cf. Bennis and Nanus 1985; Cleveland 1985a, 1985b; Cope 1988; Guskin and Bassis 1986).

Most accounts put leaders in the hero mode, attributing them

*Personal communication, 1987.

with ideas and visionary genius and indicating they have a determining effect on the behavior of others. Consistent with this view, the college president is the most important figure in the life of the institution (Kauffman 1984; Kerr 1982). Many of the cases in the next section illustrate the importance of the chief educational officer, whether president, dean, chair, or academic vice president.

Based on a study of 90 leaders in business, government, education, music, and other fields, however, the concept of leadership is broadened, linked to vision, although with regard to the origin of ideas:

> *Historians tend to write about great leaders as if they possessed transcendent genius, as if they were capable of creating their visions and sense of destiny out of some mysterious inner resource. Perhaps some do, but on closer examination it usually turns out that the vision did not originate with the leader personally but rather from others* (Bennis and Nanus 1985, p. 95).

The arrival of Harold Williams to assume the deanship of the UCLA Graduate School of Management illustrates the point. According to Williams, "It was really the faculty that brought together the concept of what it is we ought to do. They had the vision" (p. 95). Thus, "the leader only rarely [is] the one who conceive[s] of the vision in the first place. Therefore, the leader must be a superb listener, particularly to those advocating new or different images of the emerging reality. . . . Successful leaders . . . are *great askers,* and they pay attention" (p. 96).

The model in figure 1 favors this same form of leadership: The appropriate leader is a "team leader," encouraging a culture and climate in which mutual influence is respected about where an institution should be going and how it should shape itself for and during the journey (Guskin and Bassis 1986).

Direction Finding and Shaping
Using metaphors of compass and clay, the left side of the model emphasizes direction finding, the right side shaping.

Risk is associated with direction finding—with movements in the environment, with planning strategies. More risk is involved when the enterprise does not have control—and most enterprises have little control in their environments. The left side of the model is therefore about risk.

The right side of the model is about shaping the enterprise to keep it fit and efficient—running well. Less or no risk in involved in reshaping the structure, in reward systems, in control systems, and in the set of values referred to today as "organizational culture." Little risk is involved in clarifying relationships among units in an organization's structure, or in developing fairer reward systems, or in tightening the system of accounting, or in emphasizing the importance of the organization's culture.

It is contended that most of the confusion today in understanding the strategic concept is because too few practitioners and too few researchers make the distinction between the uses of compass and clay.

Strategic Thinking
The otherwise separate, fuzzy concepts of planning, management, and leadership are frequently joined in what is called the "strategic form of thinking" (see Chaffee and Tierney 1988; Cope 1988; Drake 1986; and especially Ohmae 1982).

Josh Owen, director of a higher education administrative training institute at the University of New South Wales, provides this definition of strategic thinking:

> *Strategic Thinking involves asking the question:* Where *does my institution want to go? Operational Planning is concerned with answering the question:* How *should my institution get there? Combining these two aspects, I define*

TABLE 2
THE PROPOSED LANGUAGE OF STRATEGY

Strategic	Nonstrategic
Doing the right things	*Doing things right*
Formulation	Implementation
What	How
Where	How
Ends	Means
Vision	Plans
Effectiveness	Efficiency
Strategizing	Planning

FIGURE 2
STRATEGIC TRIANGLE FOR INTEGRATING THE
THINKING OF PLANNING, MANAGEMENT,
AND LEADERSHIP

LEADERSHIP

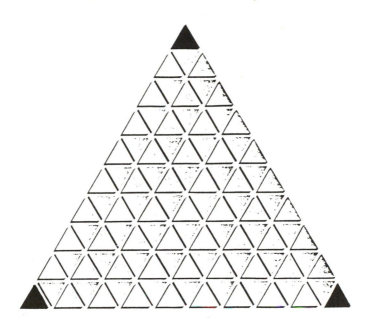

PLANNING   MANAGEMENT

Source: Ohmae 1982.

Strategic Thinking as the process of developing a vision of
where the institution wants to go and then developing man-
aging strategies [plans] on how to get there (in Hoadley and
Zimmer 1982, p. 16).

Notice the addition of "plans" to Owen's statement. To reduce the all-too-prevalent overuse of the term "strategy," it is
recommended that "strategy," "strategic," "strategizing,"
and other variations of the root word "strategy" be used exclu-
sively with the left side of the model, primarily because the ac-

quisition of resources (money, students, faculty) is more directly related to strategic choices made for direction finding relative to the resource-providing ecosystem. The use or modification of the resource follows its acquisition. Once acquired, the resources are employed to shape the institution. This left/right distinction is illustrated more completely by the "bipolar terms" in table 2.

Those who distinguish in an analytical process between "doing the right things" and then "doing things right" use the same bipolar terms. Doing the right thing is getting properly positioned in the environment. Finding the right niche is getting positioned strategically. Determining means to get to the appropriate niche is tactics or operations or simply doing things right—a restatement of the "what-or-how" or "ends-or-means" arguments applied to the strategic concept (Drucker 1974, 1985).

The complete formulation for doing the "right things right," from strategic planning as formulation to management planning as implementation, with leadership providing integration, may be expressed as a strategic thinking triangle (see figure 2). Strategic planning is, was, and always will be a way of *thinking* (Chaffee and Tierney 1988).

The cases in the next section illustrate different approaches to the process of strategic thinking; thus, they emphasize the left sides of tables 1 and 2 and figure 1. Yet as the triangle's greater complexity suggests, "formulation and implementation merge into a fluid process of learning through which creative strategies evolve" (Mintzberg 1987, p. 66). Strategic planning is in essence and at its best an idea-driven, intellectual pursuit, involving at least creativity, leadership, vision, and wisdom.

CASES IN CONTEXT

This section illustrates the strategic concept in action. The case examples are from a wide variety of institutions: from a community college to a major state university, from a college in a public university to a small, distinguished private university. Some case examples represent complex processes; others are quite simple.[1]

Given the complexity inherent in all that may be taken into account to undertake strategic planning or whole-system planning, the task for those wishing to implement a strategic concept is challenging (Bennis and Nanus 1985): This is an era marked with rapid and spastic change. The problems of organizations are increasingly complex. There are too many ironies, polarities, dichotomies, dualities, ambivalences, paradoxes, confusions, contradictions, contraries, and messes for any organization to understand and deal with (p. 8).

The following cases describe how colleges and universities have nevertheless attempted to respond to the known complexities. Each case is presented to illuminate structure, (what office, function, and staff were involved) process (the steps followed), and outcome(s) (what choices were made and with what results). Each case has a context as well, for context frequently determines the best structure and process. Each case illustrates the application of one or more attributes frequently found in applying the strategic concept. Each case is presented in approximately the same way: first a guide as to what to look for, then a description of context, a description of how the institution went about what it called strategic planning, and finally some illustration of the results.

Each case has a context as well, for context frequently determines the best structure and process.

Sometimes the institution can be identified, but in other cases, the institution is not revealed for a strategy frequently is best kept secret. For example, a large private institution, identified in this section as Center-Right University, has developed a cornerstone strategy to keep larger-scale, four-year, public institutions out of its prime market. Publicly, Center-Right University promotes the idea that it fully *serves* its prime market; privately, the staff knows its actions are to *secure* its position in that market.

1. Other cases abound in the literature. See, for example, Chaffee and Tierney (1988), Cope (1978), Keller (1983), Pailthorp (1986), Steeples (1986), and the forthcoming work of the National Center for Postsecondary Governance and Finance under the direction of Frank Schmidtlein. See also Meredith, Lenning, and Cope (1988).

What the cases have in common is usually the creation of a document that says, "The world is changing and we must too." Sometimes that document is written by an individual, such as University of Minnesota President Robert Keller's "Commitment to Focus" (1985); sometimes it is the result of a group effort, such as *Academic Prospectus*, prepared at Bradley University by the steering committee for strategic planning. Such documents usually contain summaries about changing demographics, economics, politics, and technologies and then either propose a set of directions for the future (Keller, for example) or describe a process for determining direction (Bradley University).

In every case known to the author, the entity's chief educational officer (CEO)—president, dean, or chair—creates a special, temporary committee or task force that is usually given a specific "strategic" title, such as "The Strategic Planning Committee," or a generic policy title, such as "Academic Policy Committee." Even when a standing committee for "big decisions" already exists, the newness of the strategic concept appears to call for a new group.

That group is usually charged with the responsibility to recommend ways to "carry the institution into the 21st century." George Keller's *Academic Strategy* (1983) is frequently assigned reading, along with documents on what is changing in the world around the institution. The membership always appears representative of the faculty, usually includes administrators and students, and sometimes includes trustees and alumni.

An all-campus or similar special session is usually held for the academic community in which the CEO charges the committee with the responsibility to perform admirably in its deliberations, to communicate widely, and to finish its work by a certain date, all of it frequently based on a previous resolution from the board of trustees requesting a report. The committee usually goes off on a retreat to start its work. Frequently, an advisor from outside the institution is invited to recommend ways to proceed.

Most processes begin when a substantial change has occurred within the institution (a new president) or, more often, in the environment: a downturn in the state economy, a threat from a competing institution, time for reaccreditation, or impetus from the state coordinating board seeking to define mission and role. In the last instance, strategic planning is usually done to defend the institution from the dictates of the state agency.

Most processes should result in improved strategic frameworks for addressing the future opportunities and threats in anticipated environments (see, for example, Carnegie-Mellon University and Millikin University). Some processes have limited objectives, such as the department-by-department academic program reviews at Bradley University. Some processes have ongoing strategic objectives, such as those in the example from Edmonds Community College.

The first case illustrates a simple structure and process for starting strategic planning; the following case fills in more content. The remaining cases illustrate a variety of approaches, some simple, some more complex. Woven within the cases are descriptions of strategic/contextual planning models.

Iowa State University: A New President, A State Needing Economic Development

What to observe and learn from this case

This case involves a very simple model for getting started with the strategic concept: the Strengths + Opportunities (S + O) Model (Cope 1988).[2] It assumes that an enterprise's best set of strategic choices (or key success factors) results from a combination of salient strengths leveraged on opportunities.

Note also at least two driving forces in the context (a new president and a governor emphasizing the role of higher education in economic development); how faculty were involved before the retreat, which was for administrators, and how they were then involved at the retreat; that "opportunities" are defined as conditions "out there" in the external environment; and finally that everyone was challenged to work toward a strategic framework—the structure or at least a set of understandings that allows the institution to fulfill its mission while competing successfully for resources in future environments.

Context

Throughout the early and mid-1980s, the midwestern farm economy was in serious decline, and Iowa was in the midst of the worst conditions. Iowa State University's CEO, Robert Parks, was to retire after over 20 years as president. During his tenure, the university moved from emphasizing primarily science and technology to becoming a broad-based university;

---

2. It is, in fact, the basis for the title of this monograph.

new colleges in business and design and new institutes with international orientations had been created. Iowa State University, for a long time in the shadow of the University of Iowa, was on the move. The question became "Where are its next moves?"

Further, Governor Terry Branstad exempted colleges and universities from budget cuts and even proposed adding funds for technology development to a lean state budget. It was 1986.

Process

Executive Vice President George Christensen, wanting to help the incoming CEO get off to a good start, arranged to have a one-day on-campus, strategy planning retreat for all the 130 or so senior campus administrators.

The retreat was preceded by a series of hosted luncheon meetings for about 60 faculty members in groups of five or six. They were to come up with ideas on what to do to "make ISU an even stronger university in the years ahead." Their ideas were recorded, summarized, and presented at the retreat by a member of the faculty.

The retreat started with a slide presentation by two distinguished faculty economists on the status of Iowa in a world context. The what-to-do ideas from the faculty luncheons were shared next, setting the stage for an hour of small-group discussions. Half the participants discussed the salient, internal strengths of ISU; the other half discussed the external opportunities. By the end of the morning, individual groups were able to report on ISU's primary strengths and key opportunities.

One primary salient strength was clearly the large collection of scientists in the biological sciences, both on the campus and working in many government and private laboratories in and near Ames. And one key opportunity was the worldwide attention given to the potential of biogenetics.

Lunch featured a presentation of case examples of strategic frameworks that had evolved at other institutions, including Carnegie-Mellon University and Rensselaer Polytechnic Institute. Each case example illustrated how internal strengths were related to external opportunities.

During the early afternoon, participants returned to their same tables and were challenged to relate ISU's salient strengths (where they had a comparative advantage) to key opportunities. This arrangement established a competitive atmosphere in which each table tried to come up with strategic frameworks at least as good as those presented during lunch. The "goodness" of each framework depended on how well it related to the morning's interpretation of primary strengths and key opportunities.

During the late afternoon, tables reported their conception of the best strategic framework for ISU. All participants voted on "goodness" by a show of hands as each set of ideas was presented. The results were recorded.

A "direction of travel," for example, that received a large number of endorsements included more clearly linking ISU's impressive strengths in the biological sciences and technologies to the state's economic development in a larger world context. Specific examples of how to implement this direction of travel became parts of the reporting: become more involved in the International Trade Center under construction in Des Moines, create "international professorships," and assist in the governor's proposal to build a new biotechnology research center—of course on the ISU campus.

Initial outcome

The day ended with a statement of next steps. A report on the retreat would be circulated for comments from the wider campus community, including legislative bodies, alumni, and related trade associations. Funds would be set aside to implement initiatives for the more highly endorsed strategies. Annual retreats would be held to review progress and to assess the need for redirection.

The new president then appointed a professor of economics, Jean Adams, to continue the strategic planning process. That process, with much publicity in Iowa, is under way.

The Case of the Bourbon College of Home Economics: Targeted Program Review; Assessing the Environment; Finding Direction; The Complete Process

This partially hypothetical case example illustrates a situation facing many departments and colleges of home economics. The case is built, however, upon the reality of a number of problems around the country, particularly the widely reported difficulties of the College of Home Economics at the University of Missouri (Smith 1987). While the situation presented is "hypothetical," the social, demographic, technological, and economic trends are real. The case again illustrates the simplified strategic planning process: Strength related to opportunity leads to strategic direction.[3] The process is recommended for any academic department, college, or educational organization.

What to observe

Note that the strategic concept can be related directly to any unit within the institution. The business community calls them SBUs or "strategic business units," dependent but relatively freestanding enterprises within the whole. The SBU could be a department, a college, a service, or a research unit. Note that this process is more complete yet builds upon the simple S + O Model. Note the presence of a guiding, possibly entrepreneurial, administrator or two. The driving forces in this instance are the Board of Trustees and turf warfare. Strategic planning is "demanded" as a price for survival. Note also the involvement of the outside constituency, beneficial both for ideas and for support, if necessary. This process would be ordinary academic review (or needs assessment), except that greater emphasis is placed on the external environment.

Context

The Bourbon College of Home Economics at Midwestern State University (MSU) must review its own curriculum. The university's trustees are considering the possibility of reorganizing or closing the college, and the president of the Board of Trustees is on record as having said, "There is probably no need for a college on cooking and sewing, family finance, and clothing design, given the university's new emphasis on research leading to reviving the state's rapidly declining economy." MSU's central administration has appointed a special committee and asked for the review to be completed during the next five months. A five-member, all-university review committee will make recommendations to the central administration.

The review is to involve all the college's faculty and any other stake holders the college's faculty review committee feels might contribute ideas about future directions for the college. Thus, this process involves two new, ad hoc committees: all-university and all-college. The report from the all-university re-

3. This case was used and its conclusions drawn from strategizing observations by 150 administrators attending a strategic planning workshop at the 1987 Joint Conference of the Association of Administrators of Home Economics and the National Council of Administrators of Home Economics. See Caples (1987) for a full report of the proceedings.

view will be submitted for comment to the Faculty Senate's standing Curriculum Policy Committee. The central administration will then make a recommendation to the trustees.

The decision on what to do about the College of Home Economics will be based on five criteria commonly used for program review: quality, contribution to the university's mission, need for the program, comparative advantage, and financial considerations.

The college and its mission

The broad mission of Bourbon College is its concern with helping families and individuals attain and sustain self-management, self-reliance, and control of their destiny under the broad umbrella of family and individual well-being.

The college has 30 faculty members and 525 students in three departments of about equal size: home and family living, textiles and fashion design, and foods. Because only a few new positions have been available to hire new faculty over the past 15 years and because very little turnover has occurred among existing faculty, the majority of faculty are within five years of 55 years of age. Six of the faculty are men.

Most of the students (90%) are undergraduates, and most of them are in teacher-education degree tracks. The market for teachers of home economics is declining slowly, but the college has an excellent placement record. Nearly all the students are women. Starting with the deanship of Nancy Bourbon (1939 to 1958) and continuing through subsequent deans, the college has had a strong connection with its graduates. While they contribute very little money to the college or the university, they are unusually loyal followers of college affairs and are the main reason the placement of graduates has been excellent throughout several midwestern states.

Departmental issues

The faculty in the Home and Family Living Department is especially concerned about the growing importance of "nonhuman factors" in university decisions, and they fear the possibility of their department's closing in a reorganization. The Textiles and Fashion Design Department is pleased about the review and the possibility of reorganization because it has been unsuccessful in making its case before the dean (whose background is in foods); faculty want to align the department with the Department of Chemistry and the School of Engineering, emphasizing chemical research on new textiles and the establishment of small manufacturing businesses to produce new artificial fabrics to compete with imported clothing from Asia. The Foods Department has not indicated concern with the review, feeling the dean will take care of its interests; faculty are certain the curriculum design that has served the department well for the past 20 years is adequate.

The dean's views

The respected dean, Nancy Cornmash, recently submitted an article to the leading journal of home economics about the profession's imminent death because all the other professions are moving onto its turf. Although many of her examples came from her own campus, many are found throughout North America. The faculty believed her article accurately reflected the external environment and used it as a beginning for the environmental scanning.

The article calls attention to numerous examples of encroachment taken from the journals of other professions—nurses researching the relationship between family health and nutrition and studying such matters as the effect of divorce on raising children; business schools giving advice on family investments; colleges of building and design offering courses and doing research on home construction and family sociology; colleges of natural resources emphasizing the "blue" revolution (fish farming, and fish-based diets); chemistry departments researching techniques of food preservation; a department of continuing education in cooperation with a business school developing paid-subscription, adult education courses for delivery into homes via telephones and video screens.

One example is MSU's Department of Sociology and the newly established Medical School, which are cooperating on research funded by the National Hospice Organization on how to treat the family-related effects of care for cancer and AIDS patients. She points out that the Computer Engineering Department is building experimental robots to do housework; that the Transportation Department in the Business School is studying the effect of two-earner families on home life when one commutes to work two states away; that Proctor and Gamble, the Campbell Soup Company, Nabisco Cookies, and Pepperidge Farm all have contracts with the College of Agriculture for a variety of projects related to the packaging and sale of frozen foods; and that the giants of the candy industry (Hershey, Nestle, and Mars) all have market research contracts with members of the Marketing Department in the College of Business.

She believes that "the *greatest* challenge to home economics is the challenge of interpreting in anticipated environments the relevance of the profession to others." Her article concludes that "the handwriting is on the wall" and adds, "If the profession of home economics cannot establish firmer footing on defensible turf within five years, what is known as home economics today will be history."

Strategic planning

MSU's president has suggested the college engage in strategic planning. From her alumni-supported Excellence Fund, she allocated $20,000 for planning expenses, to pay for luncheon meetings and one retreat, saying, "Strategic planning seems suited to helping a college make transitions in a changing world. When done well, the planning process will be powered by the basic need of the faculty to reexamine, to refocus, and to seek creative new ways for accomplishing their purposes."

The president suggested the starting point for determining what the college needed to do to position itself favorably for the future was to begin by examining what it already does well (its salient strengths). Then the college needed to examine economic, demographic, political, and technological changes to identify opportunities. Next, she suggested, the faculty needed to relate the strengths to emerging opportunities, resulting in a collective sense (a vision) of what the college needs to do to become outstanding.

She recommended a simplified, four-step process, with each step to take about one month (thus meeting the five-month period available to the college). The president noted that too many strategic planning processes last too long and are too often driven by unnecessary paperwork. She suggested the process should be simplified and driven by ideas.

Step one: Look inside the college. First identifying salient strengths should be emphasized: What does the college have that it can build upon? Where are the college's greatest strengths? The president suggested those involved in the planning process should think about location, reputation, values, connections to knowledge, technology, finances, physical plant, and so on. Anything the college has that it can use as leverage would be a salient strength.

The president suggested that strengths be determined by having a series of luncheon meetings involving college faculty, alumni, and invited professors from other departments. Each participant should read one or more helpful references, such as Keller (1983). The participants, however, should not forget that strategic planning is a simple idea—strengths related to opportunity—and that strategic planning is common sense.

Step two: Look outside the college. During the second month, the same groups would again meet—again over lunch—to look beyond the college. During this process, called "environmental scanning," they would look for new opportunities in the changes that are occurring. Before the luncheons, the participants read books and articles about the future by Cleveland (1985a, 1985b), Naisbitt (1982), and Toffler (1981).

Believing it is necessary for the college to at least consider the implications of several changes as well as the commitment the university has been asked to make to assist the state reverse its economic decline, the president identified several major shifts already taking place from reading the futurists: economic, technological, demographic, and social changes.

The United States is going through a transformation from an industrially based to an information-based society. The nature of work is changing. The position of the United States in world trade has changed. Patterns of employment have changed.

While more service jobs are available, there are far fewer jobs in agriculture and blue-collar industries. Research and development has created new driving technologies in microelectronics, biogenetics, lasers, fiber optics, and solar and sea exploration and exploitation.

The United State's share of world trade has been cut in half since 1950, but the number of those employed in world trade in the United States has more than doubled—from about 6 percent in the 1960s to 15 percent in the 1980s. If our share of the world market had not been cut in half, a much larger proportion of the U.S. labor force would be working in jobs directly connected to trade.

The composition of the work force has changed substantially. In 1982, 53 percent of American women were employed, compared to 38 percent of all women in 1960. Whereas 28 percent of working mothers had children under six in 1970, 45 percent of those working in 1982 had one or more children under age six.

While the economic shifts have been a source of worker displacement, blamed for the dissolution of families, and led to urban decay in smoke-stack states, people are still regarded as the most important resource in determining a nation's destiny. A considerable graying of America has occurred. In the 1950s, approximately 17 working-age people supported each social security recipient. During the 1990s, that ratio will shift to about three working-age people to one social security recipient. And by 2020 most baby boomers will be retired.

Substantial racial-ethnic shifts have occurred, with at least California, Texas, and Florida soon to enter an era when the majority of students in primary and secondary schools will be Cuban, Mexican, Southeast Asian, Korean, or Chinese.

In the 1950s, 60 percent of the family units included a father working outside the home, a homemaker mother, and two or more children. That description fits less than 10 percent of the family units today.

Step three: Propose directions of travel. During the third month, the same groups connected strengths to opportunities to recommend "directions of travel." Directions of travel might be thought of in terms of a compass. Given the many changes that cannot be controlled by the college or the university and rather than thinking a map can be made for directing travel, it is better to believe in following a path determined by a compass. The president pointed out that plans with goals and objectives are useful but pertain only to those things that can be controlled. She believed strategic planning is about only what cannot be controlled, whereas strategic management is about what is under the control of the institution: shifting internal resources, appointments, curricular offerings, and so on.

Step four: Develop a vision. Vision provides conceptual glue and momentum, and illuminates shared purpose. It provides meaning.

During the fourth month—at a retreat—all those participating in the luncheon meetings compared their "directions of travel." Everyone then worked, in small groups, to relate strengths, opportunities, and the directions of travel into a viable, visible future. At the retreat, everyone met in different small groups.

The president, drawing on Peterson's seven Rs of planning (1984), suggested using words like Redirect, Reshape, Renew,

Vision provides conceptual glue and momentum, and illuminates shared purpose.

Risk, and Reaffirm to shape direction. Given the five Rs for guidance, each group was to propose a strategic framework based upon a few directions of travel.

All participants then voted to determine the best strategic plan, identifying how strengths are related to opportunities and how the resulting directions of travel come together in a vision, to present to the All-University Review Committee. The president noted that a good plan would help her and the board *see* what the college looks like and what it would be doing five years from now. The strategic plan might include directions of travel that could involve the following elements:

1. *Redirection*: A shift toward assisting individuals in career preparation from an emphasis on serving individuals in their roles as homemakers.
2. *Redirection*: A shift from consumer protection to a preventive approach in teaching, service, and research.
3. *Reaffirmation*: Reenforcement of the importance of the multidisciplinary base of knowledge of home economics.
4. *Reshaping*: Changing the knowledge base to become more useful in health matters, especially as related to the growing proportion of elderly dependents.

The president thought this set of strategic plans (directions of travel) would result in a vision along the lines of a college's renewing its emphasis on multidisciplinary foundations while shifting resources toward health and careers and becoming proactive about preventive issues. Such a vision could satisfy the five criteria adopted by the university for program review. She also thought such a revamping would help MSU position itself more effectively in an environment emphasizing economic development.

Implementation

After the administration had an opportunity to review the college's strategic plan—probably no longer than five or six pages—the next stage of planning would move toward implementation. Each of the four elements of strategic direction (place of offering, product/program, price, and promotion) would involve annual choices, time lines, and resources.

Additional comment

This partially real case illustrates many of the practical fundamentals of strategic choice making. An "outside" force for change exists. The CEOs (president and dean) are involved. The time line is short. While the dean and president exhibit substantial leadership, involvement of other groups is also widespread. A simple model is followed. Direction-finding choices are separated from management decisions on implementation. Finally, multiple stake holders within and without the institution mean complexity and that the eventual solution will be one of finding a good enough resolution of the many interests.

Center-Right University: Strategy at Two Levels— University and College
What to observe
Note that strategic choices are best if made at two or more reinforcing levels in an organization. Note how the SBU is in a better position to make its choices when the all-institution choices are "announced." Note also that the number of strategic choices (the anticipated key success factors) is limited.

This case illustrates two main points. First, the complete process of planning involves the corporate whole *and* its constituent parts. Each academic department or program within could in turn determine its own strategic best directions; thus, the complete process is layered, starting with the corporate level. Second, it might be observed that some strategies may be kept "invisible" in a competitive environment.

Context
Center-Right University is nearly always listed among the top 10 institutions in its class: medium-size, private university. It is located in the second largest urban concentration of a northern state and is affiliated with a religious organization. It is located on one campus near the center of Northtown. The public sector is represented within a 50-mile radius only by a well-regarded, multicampus community college. The state's legislature periodically explores the possibility of building a four-year institution in Northtown, which Center-Right University perceives as a major threat.

The year before strategic planning started, the academic vice president had requested that every academic unit submit a long-range plan to take the university into the 21st century. The plans were submitted, but little sense could be made of them because they all used largely different assumptions about what was important to the university and what would happen in their external environments.

The president, academic vice president, and dean of the graduate programs decided the only way to make sense of the plans and make them coherent was to engage in strategic planning at two levels: university and school. The university, comprised of five colleges, was fiscally sound.

Structure

The CEOs created a university-level strategic planning council of about 35 members. All the members were from the faculty except the chair, the academic vice president. Each college elected five members to join a nine-member standing planning committee already appointed by the president. The Board of Trustees passed a resolution requesting a plan be submitted to them in one year. That plan would be the basis for a major capital campaign. The board's executive committee also wanted monthly updates on progress. The university's Strategic Planning Council would critique and endorse plans developed by the colleges.

Process

The director of planning served as staff for the Strategic Planning Council. The process began with a presentation by a noted expert on strategic planning practices to the full faculty. The president, vice president, and a member of the board were present to endorse the process.

A series of three one-day retreats over six weeks with the Strategic Planning Council then resulted in a university-level set of proposed plans containing four directives:

1. Serve (secure) Northtown.
2. Emphasize even more the orthodox religious tones of the institution. Move even farther to the "right."
3. Create even more options among students to move within and among the colleges. Design, for example, more graduate programs building on baccalaureate programs. (Note: This directive is not a strategic choice as defined in this report, as it does not relate to the external environment!)
4. Reduce reliance on tuition income.

Each college then went into its own series of one-day retreats, building on the university-level directions/directives.

Each retreat followed the same format: assess salient strengths, assess opportunities, determine directions of travel. For example, the 10-page report from the School of Business Administration's retreat opened this way: "The one-day retreat had modest purposes: Review the School of Business Administration's salient strengths (those providing at least some comparative advantage in the marketplace) and recommend strategic choices (directions of travel) to guide resource allocation decisions in ways (as far as possible) consistent with the four directions of the university's strategic plans."

The School of Business Administration produced four initiatives: (1) To assist in securing and serving Northtown, it would create a center for cooperative, applied business and economic research directly related to the needs of Northtown's business community; (2) to contribute to the university's religious orientation, the School of Business Administration would create an institute on poverty and ethics consistent with the university's religious orientation; (3) to enable graduates from other schools at Central-Right University to qualify for management positions in more than just business, the School of Business Administration would develop more options in the MBA program; and (4) to build on a significant strength, it would extend its already strong accounting program toward a broadened conception of information processing.

Each college came up with its own set of initiatives for review by the Strategic Planning Council. The initiatives were commented upon, sent back for further clarification, and eventually submitted to the trustees for endorsement to guide the capital campaign and to provide guidelines for budget allocations. First priority for the capital campaign and for new funds was given to those college-level initiatives consistent with the endorsed outcomes of the university-level strategic planning retreats.

Millikin University: If It's Not Broken, Don't Fix It
What to observe
While it is common for a strategic planning process to result in some innovations, perhaps even a risky move, if an audit of the situation reveals no particular problems, then the focus shifts toward what is working well.

Context
Located in Decatur, Illinois, Millikin University is usually listed in reputational studies among the top colleges in its class:

small, comprehensive universities. The central administration decided that, at its next annual retreat for administrative officers, it should review what was leading to its successes. Thus, the purpose of the review was to clarify in a "strategic" sense just what seemed to be providing this evidence of vitality: Presidents of other colleges said Millikin was among the best (*U.S. News and World Report* November 1985, October 1987); faculty salaries were increasing at rates faster than similar institutions; the numbers seeking admission were increasing; the average ACT scores of entering freshmen were increasing; job placement was very good.

Process

Only senior administrative officers attended a two-day, three-part retreat. Part one consisted of a review of current operations: admissions, indicators of success, preliminary statements about what seemed to be working well. Part two was an assessment of what was happening "out there" in demographics, economic trends, employment trends, among similar private institutions, and at the public institutions of Illinois. Part three was to address what should be done in the future.

Outcome

The retreat clarified Millikin's strategic framework and proposed no new directions. The directive to do what the institution was doing, but better, consisted of increased awareness and commitment:

1. *Maintain a lively curriculum.* Reviewers concluded that smooth faculty and administrative procedures allowed the introduction of new courses and degree programs rapidly. "An idea one year can be up and running the following year."
2. *Continue to be large* and *small.* Keep the enrollment at about 1,200. Maintain many small departments and many degree options. Innovate frequently. Support the many departments and degree options with larger-than-usual appropriations for the library and learning resource center. Continue to offer a wide range of intramural and intercollegiate sports. Support a strong fraternity and sorority system. Simply, continue to say to undergraduates, "You can get almost everything the University of Illinois has to offer in our small institution on our small campus."

3. *Continue the applied emphasis of the otherwise liberal arts curriculum.*
4. *Continue an active involvement in the social, cultural, and economic life of Decatur.* Serve that community.
5. *Maintain the present viable variety of small constituent colleges:* business, nursing, arts and sciences, and education, including the "engineering" program residing in the business school.

It should by now be clear that a strategic process can be simple, take little time, and consequently cost little. And it does not always mean change.

Carnegie-Mellon University: Keep Improving on a Viable Strategic Framework
What to observe
Carnegie-Mellon's story is a success story built on adroit presidential leadership. Carnegie-Mellon has been innovative and taken risks. Significant resources were focused in ways that might have been viewed at the outset as speculative. Note that leadership shifted over time from the strategically oriented mind of the president to widespread strategic thinking among all staff. Almost no documentation exists in the form of "strategic plans," but a vision is woven with two or three key success factors: a national university on the leading edge focusing and sharing resources.

Context
Pittsburgh's Carnegie-Mellon University, under the hand of organizational psychologist Richard Cyert, who became president in 1972, was probably the first institution to adopt the strategic planning concept. When Cyert became president, the institution was operating in the red. It was a collection of programs resulting from the 1960s merger of Carnegie Tech and the Mellon Institute.

Process
The strategic planning process started in 1972, with Cyert's proposal that every department head submit a strategic plan to the Faculty Policy Committee, a committee appointed by Cyert from "the most forward-looking professors" (Keller 1983).

Departments were reviewed one at a time. By 1974, the Faculty Policy Committee evolved into the administrator-dominated

Long-Range Planning Committee, chaired by Cyert. Some departments were closed (education) and others cut back (foreign languages), while other specific departments (computer science) or whole areas of disciplinary focus (applied social sciences) were strengthened. Every shift of resources was for the purpose of gaining comparative advantage.

A vision emerged of Carnegie-Mellon's becoming a nationally recognized professional university. According to Cyert, "The aim of strategic planning is to place a campus in a distinctive position. We must face the fact that colleges and universities are in a competitive market."

In the early years, President Cyert dominated the process, which has evolved to moving initiatives from the departments. The organizational aim has been to instill a way of thinking throughout the institution. Again according to Cyert, "The key element in strategic planning is to get everyone in the organization to think that way."

A strategic framework

Perhaps the most important lesson in the Carnegie-Mellon model is clarification over time of a "strategic framework" that defines how the structure and processes of the institution contribute to how well the institution will play the competitive game.

In the Carnegie-Mellon model, each department is expected to focus on what it does best and relate that strength to a limited number of broad themes; thus, concentrated strength (focus) is linked to themes for flexibility. Two themes, for example, are professional application and information; thus, the psychology department emphasizes cognitive processes and how the mind processes information, the mathematics department emphasizes applied mathematics, the computer science and engineering departments emphasize information through robotics, and the history department has an unusual Ph.D. program in applied history. Strength gives competitive advantage; themes allow that strength to be shared across departments among selected themes.[4]

4. An outstanding example of how the concentration of resources in a department is related to broader themes and contributes to viability is the 1978 Nobel Prize awarded Herbert Simon. Professor Simon has an appointment in the Department of Psychology, regarded as among the top five psychology departments in the country. Yet the Nobel Prize was in *economics* for how financial institutions process information.

Furthermore, to give competitive edge to strength and earn distinction, each department is to "move early into the intellectual frontiers of tomorrow."

Finally, the "framework" operates with little or no documentation of plans. Once the strategic spirit is instilled, the culture supports it. The only continuing element of process is an annual retreat to examine and reexamine strategies. Each annual retreat focuses on the activities of different stake holders: the applied institutes, the trustees, graduate programs, interdisciplinary education and research, and so on.

Other institutions have adopted variations of Carnegie-Mellon's strategic framework (see figure 3). (Because the draft statement in figure 3 is an "internal" document, the identity of the university is purposely obscured.) The left of the page identifies particular targeted disciplines. The middle column, Pro-

FIGURE 3
ACADEMIC PLANNING FRAMEWORK
OF DISTINCTIVE UNIVERSITY

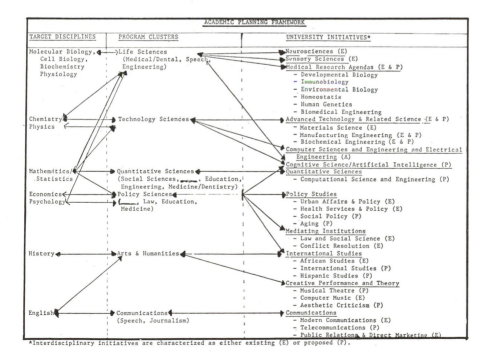

gram Clusters, is somewhat like the themes of Carnegie-Mellon. The final column identifies specific initiatives. Together, they make a framework. A quotation from the university's *Plan for Distinction* demonstrates how this university's strategic thinking drives interpretation:

> *Economics is identified as a pivotal social science. It is distinctive for the breadth of its theory and the rigor of its methodology. This unit is already strong at [this university] and contributes to work in the professional school of management, as well as policy-related research and education. It also affords a framework for collaboration with law, education and social policy, and medicine* (internal document).

The University of Minnesota:
A Big Institution Moves Slowly
What to observe
The difficulties at the University of Minnesota are no doubt the result of many factors: It is among the largest universities in the world; recent presidents have pushed a top-down model of strategic planning; little actual participation has occurred; outside stake holders can focus on the single giant; the legislature forced system-wrenching retrenchments twice during the process—and so on. Observe that a strategic process may last many years through many study groups and many reports. Valuable changes in the way resources are allocated may not be any more obvious than the quality of strategic thinking that takes place slowly throughout the institution.

Context
Among the largest institutions in the nation, the University of Minnesota also has had one of the longest experiences with the strategic concept. The strategic concept was initially introduced there by President Magrath in the mid-1970s.

Process
In the beginning—and largely continuing—the process was almost completely top down, with Magrath's writing a mission statement and creating a planning council to begin a comprehensive planning process. The Planning Council argued for three years about how the university should plan (Keller 1983), inviting leading planners and financial analysts to campus for

one-day, how-to-plan seminars. A major conclusion after the three years was that the university should have 40 bottom-up planning units and that each should plan its own strategy.

During the late 1970s and early 1980s, the 40 units came up with individual five-year plans. Typical of such efforts, the plans tended toward the optimistic and grandiose—mere wish lists. Then the legislature twice—in 1980 and 1981—required the university to return large sums, upward of $60 million, to the general fund. The emphasis turned to retrenchment, mostly across the board. A growing awareness of costs translated itself into cost comparisons with other similar programs across the campus and across the nation. "Strategic planning turned out to have some teeth in it and succeeded in significantly shifting resources (Clugston 1987, p. 153). Those resources—at least in the College of Arts and Sciences—shifted to departments ranked high on quality from departments ranked low.

Perhaps little more was gained during those difficult years that translated much beyond survival strategies for retrenchment. Important, however, was the growing awareness of the need to begin planning institutionwide and laterally, with new processes, that attempted to provide for more attention to the external environment and to such matters as comparative advantage and how to get it.

The Magrath presidency and the budget cuts paved the way for the presidency of Robert Keller. In 1985, while interim president, Keller wrote the cornerstone of the current strategic planning efforts, a 22-page document called "Commitment to Focus." Basically, the document calls for the university to focus resources, become 8,000 students smaller over about six years, and become firmly ranked among the top five public universities in the nation.

This document clearly sets direction. It was followed by a document entitled "A Strategy for Focus," which laid out guidelines for future program development that, for example, explained that increased resources would not be based upon increases in *size* but on program *changes*. "A Strategy for Focus" represents a shift in orientation for program development at the University of Minnesota: *Growth* in resources is not the primary means to improve programs; *change* is the primary means to improvement.

The beginning of implementation was a 144-page document produced by a faculty advisory committee, *Plan to Focus* (June 1987). The report contained 238 specific recommendations; two

Important was the growing awareness of the need to begin planning institutionwide and laterally, with . . . more attention to the external environment.

of the recommendations called for the closing of two schools. A storm of protest resulted. The regents refused to follow those particular recommendations.

In September 1987, the Academic Affairs Planning Committee (largely a committee of senior administrators) prepared another "background paper," describing the basis for future university planning. This document is largely a restatement of Keller's "Commitment to Focus" with more operational guidelines that build on some of the major recommendations of the *Plan to Focus*.

Comment

The University of Minnesota's attempt at strategic planning demonstrates the difficulties of moving a massive, loosely coupled organization set in a political landscape. Citizens, the governor, and the legislature all watch the institution. Some observers inside and outside believe it is moving too fast; others believe it is moving too slow. It appears that centrally directed decision-making guidelines are becoming accepted. For example, comparative advantage, demand, centrality, quality, and efficiency are becoming the accepted criteria for program review.

Decision making among departments is becoming more important. More lateral thinking is occurring. Dozens of piecemeal strategies are blending into more of a federal union, with, for example, requirements that lateral departments become involved in new faculty appointments. Needs of the Medical School are more clearly expressed in appointments in the Department of Biology.

Outside pressures and better management appear to be bringing about more external, farsighted thinking about the whole enterprise. But progress is slow. For large, multi-divisional organizations, this way may be obligatory. For such institutions, it may be possible to manage change in seemingly small ways: Discussion documents, awareness sessions, new processes, new criteria, small interventions added to natural organizational forces add up over time.

Perhaps this example is the most valuable one of attempted application of the strategic concept for the past 10 or so years. It is valuable in its lengthy history of attempts to move a large institution by central administration. The story is still being written, however.[5]

Bradley University: A Finely Tuned
Program Review Process
What to observe
This case illustrates the use of the strategic concept in cross-campus departmental review. Note that two of the key criteria are external (demand and comparative advantage) and three are internal (quality, centrality, and cost). Note how the faculty approved the process at the outset, because of the probable consequences of the review, and note that a temporary steering committee started the process and proposed the model to the faculty.

Context
Bradley University, in Peoria, Illinois, recognized it was in the center of a state anticipating a decline by approximately one-third in the number of students graduating from high schools. Furthermore, largely because of the declining fortunes of the Caterpillar Company, the local economy was severly depressed. It was 1981. The university's administration, largely at the urging of Academic Vice President John Hitt, adopted the strategic planning concept. The cornerstone of the effort would be program review, academic and nonacademic.

Process
A four-member steering committee of faculty and administrators was appointed to recommend a planning process to the Faculty Senate. The steering committee prepared a document, *An Academic Prospectus*, which reviewed the history of the institution and placed that history into the then-current environment. A major point was that difficult decisions were required to preserve the institution's viability. At that point, the president, vice president, and members of the steering committee arranged to visit with the faculty in every academic department, one at a time, over a six-week period. Each visit provided an opportunity to discuss the situation of the university and the needs of the departments.

5. For more details on the University of Minnesota, see Baker 1982; Clugston 1986, 1987; Hearn and Heydinger 1985; and Keller 1983.

A companion document proposed a detailed plan to review every department. The details of the plan to review all departments included a set of five criteria now frequently used by universities for academic reviews (see Cope 1981; Smith 1987): four primary criteria of quality, centrality, demand, and comparative advantage and the additional criterion of cost/efficiency.

The plan also provided for the creation of a 14-member strategic planning committee with faculty members elected by the Faculty Senate and administrators appointed by the president. The first responsibility of the committee was to review all academic and nonacademic departments, considering the same criteria. It was clear some departments might be closed, others restructured. The Faculty Senate approved the plan.

The department heads—from Admissions to Zoology—were asked to provide evidence of performance, using the four primary variables. Costs were computed separately. All the evidence was reviewed, and the Strategic Planning Committee voted separately on perceived performance on each primary criterion on a five-point scale from "very strong" to "very weak." For example, the Department of Economics received the highest ratings for centrality and quality but somewhat lower ratings for demand and comparative advantage. The highly regarded Admissions Office received top ratings in each category.

Outcome

More than 60 academic and over 50 nonacademic departments were rated. As a direct result of the review, about six academic departments were closed or merged with others; a similar number of nonacademic departments were reorganized.

Caring Arts College: A Complete, Structured Model Applied to Enhance Strategic Thinking
What to observe

This example illustrates a logical learning process from review of mission to plans for implementation. That process is supported by a six-step, contextual planning model (Cope 1985a). Learning is stressed in this case. Because the faculty and most administrators in this institution had little real experience in thinking about how to plan for the institution's future and because one of the goals was to implant a continuing capacity to plan, the planning committee was taken through a thorough, step-by-step, strength-by-strength, reasoned planning process. One goal was learning; the other was to make strategic choices.

Also note that the model does not address weaknesses until the stage of implementation—step six. See the extended commentary at the end of this case, which explains why institutional weaknesses are properly, but not usually, addressed late in the process.

Context

The church-related Caring Arts College, located near the center of one of the nation's larger cities, obtained a Title III planning grant, hired a director of planning, created a 13-member strategic planning committee (students, faculty, administrators, and trustees), and spent 18 months in a planning process. That process followed six steps in the model for contextual planning (see Cope 1985a).

Process

The first step of the model (see figure 4) requires a review of mission. Step 2 is a determination of salient strengths, one at a time. Step 3 is a situation analysis of each strength whose purpose is to look for evidence that that strength might be eroded, either by a market trend or the actions of competitors. Step 4 is a reassessment of each strength according to how well it has been deployed and how it may be deployed to greater advantage in the future. Step 5 is a complete statement of intended strategy. Step 6 moves the strategy into implementation.

The Strategic Planning Committee went on a one-day or a two-day retreat to conclude each step. Between steps, task forces worked on particular issues, gathered additional information, or simply communicated to stake holders (trustees to trustees, faculty to faculty, and so on).

The committee concluded that the mission had three emphases: to convey the liberal arts, to prepare students for careers, and to imbue students with the special caring and humanitarian flavor of human relations so much a part of campus life and a cornerstone of the religious order that had originally established the college to educate Catholic women. (Men had been admitted 10 years earlier.)

Step 2 determined, partly through market studies, that the institution's salient strengths included its central location in a favored residential portion of the city near excellent transportation, parks, and museums. Other strengths included strong

FIGURE 4

CONTEXTUALLY ORGANIZED PARTICIPANT
ENCOUNTERS (C.O.P.E.) MODEL

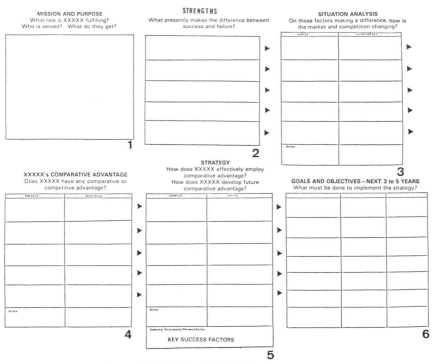

Source: Adapted from South 1981.

departments preparing individuals to work with the handicapped, its particular site and beautiful campus, a dedicated faculty, and a quality image.

Step 3 assessed each strength individually to determine any actual or potential erosion. For example, it was determined that the college's locational advantage was being eroded in two ways: the competing six or seven institutions—mostly in the suburbs—were nearly all setting up annex operations in Caring Arts College's "backyard"; in addition, the students traditionally served were moving to the suburbs as the inner city continued its decades-long decay. On the other hand, the strength of programs related to the handicapped was not being eroded by competition, and the general market was becoming more favorable as increased federal and state attention was given to the needs and rights of the handicapped. Telephone surveys done by an independent firm indicated the college's quality image was on the wane. Each of six strengths was similarly assessed.

During step 4—retreat 4—each strength was again examined one at a time and tentative conclusions reached: Make better use of the advantage of location by illustrating it with maps in publications, using nearby museums in course requirements, promoting the good transportation system to the nearby business community and to parents of present students who could attend evening continuing education programs; start an advertising program to shore up the waning image.

During step 5, it was decided to adopt a two-phase strategy. During the three-year first phase, selective strengths (education to care for the handicapped, location, site, faculty) would be built so that in the three-year second phase, a substantial move upward, from nearer the lower end of the range among competing institutions to among the top third, could be made on tuition. One matter was not resolved: Should a branch campus, largely to serve adults, be established in the suburbs? Later it was decided to do so.

In step 6, after many meetings between the heads of functions and members of the Strategic Planning Committee, a complete set of plans for implementation was proposed and endorsed. For example, convince the trustees of another Catholic institution that its tuition level was also too low: "Move up to make room for us." Other conclusions were that the business studies program should be trimmed somewhat to provide additional resources for the college's traditional strength in education to care for the handicapped, that a more aggressive promotional program linked to a development initiative was required, and that the business office should attempt to lease office space in one of the residence halls to raise funds specifically to enhance the caring and humanistic attributes of campus life (improved student lounges, comfortable chairs and lamps for faculty offices, for example).

Additional observations
The model shown in figure 4 provides an orderly process for structuring the interpretation of information and choosing among alternatives. Some authorities oriented toward psychology suggest all models should be like psychotherapy: The solution (correct behavior) is within the collective person (the organization); therefore, the model is a facilitator (therapist)

helping the group (the enterprise) find the right solution (appropriate strategy) to her or his own problem.

The contextual planning process imbedded in this model is a decision-making/learning process. First and foremost, contextual planning provides for a shared interpretation or meaning. It is also an organized, encountering process. The participants learn a conceptual approach to frame the variety of variables in the institution's context.

Participants propose, evaluate, and choose a solution to the "problem" situation. They learn what is relevant and how to use the information they collect. In this process of participation, they become more committed to their own institution's directional paths.

Caring Arts College followed the observation that weaknesses are handled best during implementation rather than during the formulation of strategy (Steiner 1979b). For example, if weaknesses had been addressed early in the process, one weakness would have been the lack of the latest computer technology in the business program. Because business (high tech) was to be deemphasized and the caring, humanitarian atmosphere (high touch) emphasized, homey lamps and comfortable chairs were more important than more computer stations.

It seems appropriate to address weaknesses only in the context of implementing an already-agreed-upon set of key success factors. For example, Caring Arts College seeks to increase the proportion of men on campus from 15 percent to about 25 percent. Doing so will require more male-related provisions—from bathrooms to sporting activities. But more bathrooms and more sporting activities will assist in the achievement of the "positioning" strategy: to increase the attractiveness of Caring Arts College and make it more like other coeducational colleges.

Another reason for addressing weaknesses later in connection with agreed-upon strategic direction is that an early assessment of weaknesses is devisive, while a purpose of strategic planning is to gain greater consensus. Displaying weaknesses, whether agreed upon or not, encourages division and defensive, turf-protecting behavior.

A review of mission, like addressing weakness, can be deferred until late in the process. Mission (as reviewed in step 1) is the organization's *present* purpose, position, and strategy. It results from the current mix of strengths, commitments, opportunities, and competitive forces. For the currently successful organization, mission is the wisdom of today.

While mission occupies a prominent location in the model, it is usually not fruitful to begin a strategy retreat or longer process with a review of mission. Consider instead a mission restatement—if at all—after new directions of travel are tentatively decided upon. Then see whether the new initiatives (if any) require any change in mission. Millikin University's strategy review, for example, did not require any mission revision.

Vision (as an outcome of step 5) is the *future* focus, and it should be a part of step 5. Vision grabs attention. Vision is the combination of strengths related to opportunities projected forward. Visions provide road maps that guide the implementation through what may be a tangle of complexities. Vision sets the agenda in context. Vision inspires, animates, and transforms mission into action. It is the conceptual glue. The right vision and key success factors sweep energy back and forth in subtle ways.

The first five steps in this model are the left portion of the two-part model in figure 1. Implementation (the right side of the model) might simply be conceived of as the management of vision.

The central task of the strategic process is to consolidate (as in Millikin's case) or challenge the wisdom of today (as in the mission of Caring Arts College). The process should be conceived of as a process for self-discovery, a creative process aimed at finding opportunity.

Learning

This model supports a learning process (Bennis and Nanus 1985; Mintzberg 1987). Participants develop a wider and deeper working knowledge. Eventually the institution as a whole, through the increased capacity of its staff to think strategically, builds a strategic framework of tuition, degree options, location, themes, as well as a culture of strategic thinking. This process is institutional learning. Participants learn a conceptual approach and a knowledge-organizing framework for focusing on a variety of variables in a given situation; they can generate and redesign strategic solutions. They learn what to focus upon and learn how to determine strategic direction consistent with mission, strengths, competition, and the institution's culture.

Historical perspective

Furthermore, an accurate learning process is reinforced still further if the process is couched in a historical perspective. As there is much to learn—and much to choose—from among contemporary events, the institution's history adds perspective. History gives a view of organizational development that is more accurate than the one obtained by seeing such matters only in the present. Participants need a broad canvas to account for the past and to project well into the future. Therefore, it is often recommended that a strategic planning retreat begin with a slide show history of the institution, including old pictures of buildings, students, employees, laboratories, locations, and so on.

Then the process can begin with a mission review (if it is not simply a fiction) or an assessment of strengths.

Leadership

The leader who plans contextually relies on expressions of history, of intuitive, felt, or tacit knowledge—the substances of self-discovery. The strategy of the actors is choice based on layers of values and interpreted realities. These values can only be known by the participating actors (faculty, administrators, and so on)—at least initially—in the manner of tacit knowing.

The contextual leader elects to make the actors themselves the primary data-gathering and information-interpreting instruments, because the actor-as-instrument, although not perfect (in fact, messy), is infinitely insightful and adaptable. The result is a strategic framework consistent with the realities and values of the participants.

Southwest Joint Center for Education: The Straw Model for Planning

What to observe

This case presents an exception to the orientation toward participatory self-discovery of most of this report. Because time is short or many factions are involved, a consulting facilitator may be called in to undertake strategic planning, which happened in this case. Sometimes a straw model is useful to get consensus.

This case discusses the "issues approach" to formulating strategy. An issues approach usually begins by listing a set of problems/issues that need to be resolved in planning: adequate salary levels, state or federal government initiatives, general education, faculty morale, role of the faculty senate, and so on.

Commonly, task forces address each issue and report to the whole group. An issues approach might have been the model to use for the Southwest Joint Center, but time precluded its use.

It is often recommended that a strategic planning retreat begin with a slide show history of the institution.

Context

The Southwest Joint Center for Education in Washington state was proposed by a coalition of business, political, and community interests in 1983 to deliver education and training related to economic development for southwestern Washington. Four existing colleges were joined in a collaborative enterprise: a state university, a four-year public college, and two community colleges. By 1986, after three years of operation, the need was apparent to look into the future. How were the four institutions to cooperate? How were emerging high-technology industries to be served? How were local school districts and the community to be served?

The management group in this instance was the politically influential Advisory Council, whose membership included four state legislators, four representatives of leading firms in the area, four representatives of the cooperating institutions, four representatives of the community at large—one of whom was considered the "father" of the original idea—and two representatives from local school districts. Director and political scientist George Condon was responsible for the center's daily management. According to Condon, "The political, demographic, and economic forces operating in this instance were substantial."

The opportunity for economic development in the area is great (see figure 5). The location is at a significant transportation hub. This area—along with the Panama Canal region—is probably the least developed area with so much potential for transportation on the entire east shore of the Pacific from Alaska to the tip of South America. It has open land, a new interstate bridge across the navigable Columbia River connecting the site to an international airport, and an emerging high-technology industry. It is also a desirable location from the standpoint of recreational opportunities and climate. It is a good place to live, and substantial numbers of people are moving north from Portland. The area has obvious opportunities for further business expansion, with its rare minerals, water quality, low power rates, land, transportation, and location on the Pacific Rim.

Both major state universities were potential actors as well.

MAP 1

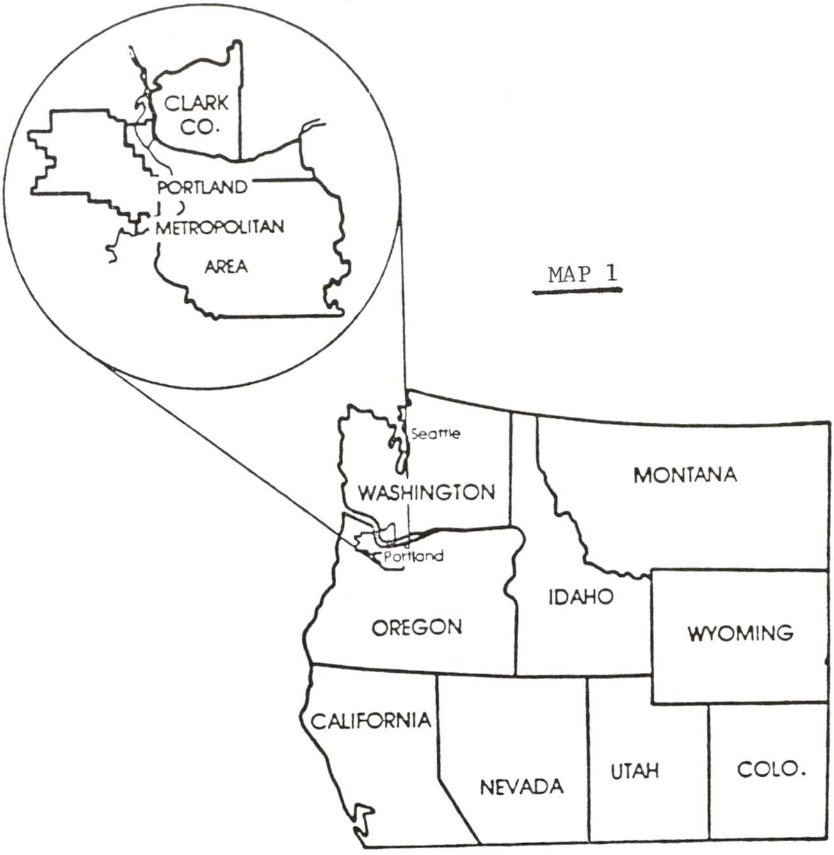

The University of Washington in Seattle is a leading annual contender for federal grants and positions itself as the flagship university within the region, while Washington State University, already "positioned" among the four cooperating schools, seeks to be *the* state university. One of the cooperating colleges (Evergreen State College) was showing signs of leaving the consortium because its faculty strategic planning committee wanted to concentrate resources on its main campus, 60 miles to the north.

Governor Booth Gardner and the state legislature were con-

FIGURE 5 (continued)

**TWO VIEWS OF AN IMPORTANT LOCATION ON THE
EAST SHORE OF THE PACIFIC OCEAN**

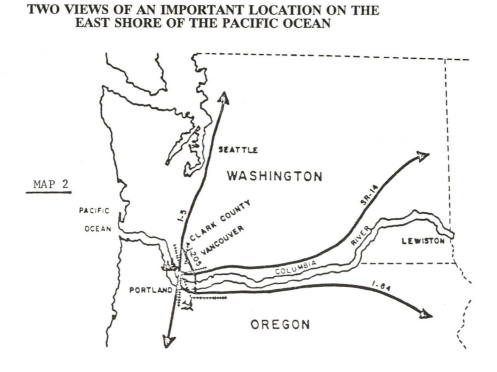

tenders for the honor of which was doing more for economic development by encouraging new business and by reforming the common school system while developing higher education.

Thus, the stage was set for contention.

Process

In a case with many competing interests, a general technique is to create a series of "strawman" models, each a potential strategic solution to the problem at hand.

First a strawman model solution is created that contains all points of view from all the interested parties (the stake holders); then a second and a third and a fourth model are created. Each model gets closer to one that stake holders will eventually agree upon. [See Hart et al. (1985) for more insights into how this model works.]

The process is one of first letting stake holders know that they will see a series of straw models and that they will critique each in turn. Creating the models is best accomplished by interviewing and then meeting in a group. During the interviews, the pieces of the model are constructed; during the group meetings, the critique takes place and stake holders bargain/negotiate in public. Figure 6 outlines the general process.

The first round, from introductory meeting to first critique, should take about a week to a month; after that point, new models and critiques should take place about every week. The whole process, to the point of reaching agreement, should take about two months—certainly no more than three—and require about five meetings among stake holders.

Additional Comment

To keep the process "strategic," it is necessary to remind stake holders of the environmental forces involved, so it is a prominent part of the first and every meeting. The "goodness" of each model is then critiqued emphasizing the play of environmental forces, not the interests of the factions.

In this case, participants agreed that it was desirable to invite Washington State University to become the dominant player among cooperating institutions and to expand graduate offerings, but not to develop anything specifically like a research park for the time. The structure of governance was rearranged slightly.

The issues approach

Sometimes institutions follow an issues approach to strategic planning. Usually faculty groups are assigned to report back to the administration or to the faculty government on each issue after a retreat or some months later if task forces are involved. The issues approach has its problems, however.

The main problem revolves around seeing the whole view quickly. The issues approach may lack the capacity to bring about a common view on the necessarily integrated set of key success factors. For example, *Strategic Decision Making*, a recent publication for trustees (Frances et al. 1987), lists 42 strategic issues, from the need to ensure sound financial management to changing mission as necessary to match changes in the external environment. Each issue represents a critical decision area, and too many of the issues are limited solely to internal matters. Setting priorities is thus particularly difficult with so many issues, and issues—key decision areas—frequently get separated by working task forces. The CEO, whose attention is critical to implementation, probably cannot give sufficient at-

FIGURE 6
STEPS IN A STRAWMAN MODEL

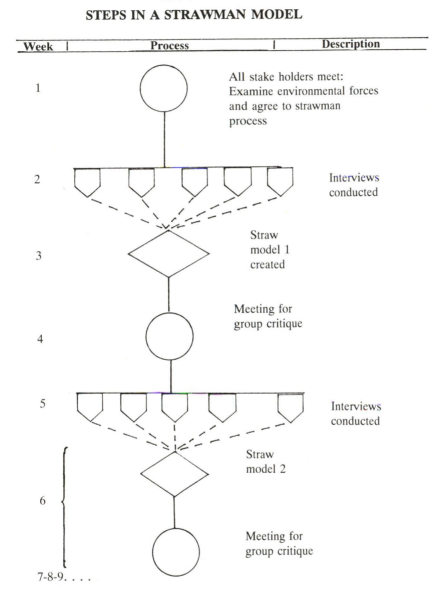

Week	Process	Description
1		All stake holders meet: Examine environmental forces and agree to strawman process
2		Interviews conducted
3		Straw model 1 created
4		Meeting for group critique
5		Interviews conducted
6		Straw model 2
7-8-9. . . .		Meeting for group critique

tention to the tasks, especially as the issues approach usually takes quite a long time to reach even a tentative conclusion—frequently 12 to 18 months.

The result of the issues approach is that apparently nothing happens. If the purpose is to forestall action while seemingly encouraging strategic planning, then the CEO or a steering group appointed by the CEO should develop a list of issues and have the usual factional interests have a go at it. One reason some campuses have found that strategic planning did not work is that they took the issues road.

College of Education, San Diego State University: Strategic Planning with Pictures
What to observe

It is necessary to keep group processes fresh. During the 1950s and 1960s, T-groups were prominent. During the seventies and early eighties, retreats with standard flip charts became the fashion. Now some strategic planning has been done with pictures. Observe in this case the importance of leaders' continuing to reinforce the importance of key success factors after strategy is formulated. Finally, as this example again illustrates how to use the S + O Model in a retreat only to the point of formulation, note how "quick starts" begin the process of implementation.

Context

Dean of Education Ann Morey wanted to formulate strategic plans in collaboration with over 100 faculty at San Diego State University. Within the California system and among institutions nationally, some of the college's programs are seen as on the leading edge.

Morey decided to ask for help from a group facilitator and a graphic designer. She arranged to have two faculty retreats, at which attendance was optional. The first retreat was for college-level directions of travel; the second focused on the departments.

In both retreats, the facilitator led the faculty as it thought through its salient strengths and considered opportunities. Small-group meetings and meetings of the whole were held. Everything said was recorded graphically in colors as it occurred. If someone said "school," it was drawn. If someone said "computer," a computer appeared on the design paper that covered the walls (see figure 7). Everyone not only heard but also saw the points developing. Soon faculty were presenting their own ideas with pictures.

For the college, the faculty decided on three "directions of travel"—three strategic directional choices emphasizing (1) multicultural learning, (2) expanded service to the urban community, and (3) applied research. The dean added her own

FIGURE 7
CONTEXTUAL PLANNING WITH PICTURES

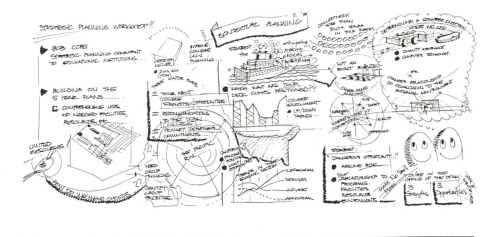

challenge to the faculty: "Dare to lead in those three directions." A design emerged. Consensus emerged. Then the sessions moved to "quick starts"—actions that could begin the
following day, week, or month.

Comment

The directions of travel—the agreed-upon design—appeared to
represent the multiple interpretations of the realities these faculty members knew as tacit knowledge. (See the later section
on the importance of visualizing, seeing the whole picture, and
tacit knowledge.) Strategic planning with pictures has been
found successful in several settings and is recommended when
the services of a designer or cartoonist are available.

Since the retreats, the dean has consistently allocated faculty
appointments, leaves, special research funds, and so on on the
basis of the faculty's three choices. This college is now one of
the most highly externally funded colleges of education on at
least the West Coast.

Edmonds Community College: A President
Getting Ahead of the Institution
What to observe

Sometimes a college does not need to discover a set of key
success factors in a planning process. In this instance—largely

because of the entrepreneurial style of the campus president—the college had already taken key initiatives, but it was necessary to affirm them. It was necessary to give the faculty an opportunity to "see the institution" as if through the "eyes" of the office of the president.

Observe too how voting contributes to a necessarily democratic process. Thus, the purpose of the retreat was less formulating a good set of strategic choices than it was an opportunity to participate and communicate. An observer of the process concluded, "Faculty representatives now have new opportunities to participate in planning, and communication has opened up between faculty and the president" (Jacob 1987, p. 8).

Context

The college is located north of Seattle near the path of a developing high-technology corridor and south of major assembly operations for the Boeing Aircraft Corporation. The college started in the late 1960s in makeshift facilities with a curriculum emphasizing jobs and the local industries (metal fabrication, fishing, wood products) before the emergence of high technology. The current president, Tom Nielson, was criticized by the largely arts-oriented faculty for an entrepreneurial style of leadership, for ignoring transfer students and the liberal arts programs at the college while he created highly visible partnerships with industry. Less than half of the college's operating funds are now provided by the state. As the college appeared to find its "corporate partner–organizational niche" (Bennis and Nanus 1985), the liberal arts faculty felt left out and demanded the creation of a college planning committee.

Process

One of the first tasks of the College Planning Committee, under the direction of Executive Vice President Jennis Bapst, was to plan a one-day strategic planning retreat. The retreat followed the simplified strategic planning model: Campus strengths related to environmental opportunity determine strategic direction. Before the retreat, his committee obtained a resolution from the trustees that the college must plan strategically.

The retreat's participants included all the trustees, the executive cabinet, all division directors, and the 13 members of the Planning Committee. About 35 people attended. The participants concluded the retreat by voting on a best proposal put forth by one of the participants. After the strengths and opportunities were pictured and reviewed (by mid-afternoon), each participant wrote her or his own set of key success factors and posted them on the walls for every other member's vote. Each participant voted twice.

A best proposal was one that had to demonstrate it was built on present strengths and was related to the opportunities "out there." The proposal obtaining near complete agreement had five directions of travel, including more emphasis on matters related to the international scene (particularly the Pacific), serving the growing presence of Naval facilities, serving business and industry, retraining needs for new technologies, and serving the needs of the less advantaged, particularly the growing proportion of senior citizens.

The picture form of image sharing was used during the retreat, as the faculty included a former professional cartoonist. The president, clearly backed by the trustees, promised that he would follow the directions set by the retreat in making decisions. The results of the retreat were shared widely by memo for additional comment; they continue to live as the Planning Committee continues its deliberations. The illustrations from the retreat were hung in the faculty dining room as a constant reminder of the directional choices endorsed.[6]

Summarizing Observations
RE: Preplanning

1. A document describing the history and current situation of the institution with an emphasis on anticipated environments is essential. It should be widely distributed.
2. The trustees should endorse the concept.
3. The chief educational officer needs to demonstrate that the process will result in guidelines that will determine how resources will be shifted.

6. In a similar retreat at Mount Union College in Ohio, the courageous—and right-thinking—president, Harold Kolenbrander, took all 18 individual statements prepared by faculty at an opportunities retreat back to the main campus for all the faculty to vote on. The set of propositions receiving the largest number of votes at the retreat was not revealed. The "at-home" faculty—after a review of the strengths and opportunities decided on at the retreat—voted again. They endorsed the same set of propositions.

RE: Content

1. Focus on opportunities in the challenges of the external environment.
2. Separate external strategic choices from internal operational decisions.
3. Concentrate on a limited number of strategic choices. Reduce complexity by recommending that groups focus on pairs of ideas. For example, move internationally and decentralize, or emphasize selected themes linked to stronger departments like computers to biological systems.
4. Emphasize the qualitative directions of travel over quantitative goals during the planning phase.

RE: Process

1. The CEO must exhibit a continuing and visible commitment.
2. Staff at all levels and from all functions should be involved.
3. Provide a modest structure like the simple models illustrated in the cases.

RE: Content of process

1. Move meetings to retreat settings. Most large-scale, big-picture considerations require new perspectives. If the setting is close to the campus, thinking will be restricted.
2. Focus on directional choices and frameworks rather than on specific outcomes. The directional choices or the strategic frameworks provide longer-term utility beyond the particular goals.
3. Recognize the professional ethos of the institution's culture. Allow participants to learn about that ethos as groups learn together.
4. Keep communications open. Allow the discussion to become larger than the agenda so all interests can be heard. Allow all issues to come out. If an issue gets in the way of the process, however, assign it to a task force.
5. Present the same information in different ways to accom-

modate different styles of perceiving. And keep the information based on numbers to a minimum.

6. Recognize that while groups are usually more effective than individuals in generating sets of ideas, individuals are often more effective in integrating those ideas in a single vision.

7. Identify "quick starts" and provide for annual reviews.

RE: Outcomes

The process should result in institutional understandings about several factors:

- *Clientele*: What needs of the potential stake holders—students, firms, other institutions, alumni, government, and so on—will be met?
- *Program mix*: What range of educational, service, research, and economic development offerings will be available from the entity?
- *Geographic service area:* What region is to be served?
- *Comparative advantage*: What position(s) will the institution occupy in the marketplace? This position should be defined particularly in regard to its strengths or special advantages relative to other institutions of higher education.
- *Basic mission*: How do the role and scope of the institution incorporate all of the above factors? The mission should be reviewed for any changes *after the process of strategizing is completed* to allow more likelihood for change to be contemplated wisely.

A mission statement consistent with what has been suggested so far in this report should (1) differentiate it from other institutions, (2) define where the institution is going rather than where it is, (3) inspire others, and (4) stand up to disagreement. Statements about "maximizing growth potential" or "providing an education of the highest quality" cannot be disagreed with and are not worth stating.

Finally, the results of a strategic planning process should provide participants with the glimmer of something perhaps improbable, surely difficult, and maybe even remote.

FUNDAMENTALS OF APPLICATION

This section explores fundamentals of applying the strategy concept. The range of homegrown, innovative practices among colleges is already substantial and admirable, and the techniques illustrated next should add to the richness of further applications.

It is contended, however, that one of the major shortcomings in the application of the strategic concept has been the lack of awareness of the concept's rich heritage. A lack of understanding is apparent. Those foundations are the subject of the last section. The serious student of the strategy concept needs definitions, cases, and experience with applications *and* will eventually want to think deeply about the concept's historical and theoretical origins. First, however, this section contributes additional perspectives on the practices seen in the case examples of the previous section.

Those applying the strategic concept will find it valuable to differentiate between directional planning and internally directed managerial decisions. They will also develop a deeper understanding of the environment as ecosystem, determine that for effectiveness it is necessary only to achieve a "satisficing" level of accomplishment with our necessarily loosely coupled institutions, and adopt other matters—such as participative management—that are related to leadership and organizational behaviors (Chaffe and Tierney 1988; Cope 1981, 1985a, 1988; Norris and Poulton 1987). Much of this section addresses these interrelated concepts (which are also part of the primary model illustrated in figure 1).

The concept of "loosely coupled" is fundamental to how the academic organization is perceived. What is an academic organization? For the purposes of this report, stressing as it does people and ideas, an academic organization *is* people and ideas (Chaffee and Tierney 1988; Cope 1988; Peterson 1980; Peterson et al. 1986). An organization is a culture made up of needs, values, sagas, history, and future direction. An organization is a constructed entity, negotiated, renegotiated, and created by participants in given contexts.

An academic enterprise, saturated as it is with professional expertise, is viewed as a loosely coupled and loosely bound assortment of people sharing some common reason for collective action in an environment. Our academic enterprises are thus taken to be democratic cultures existing in a resource-providing ecosystem (Cleveland 1985b).

The remainder of this section recommends fundamentals this

There is no question about the importance of sharp arrows, but concentrating on arrow sharpening leads to starvation.

loosely coupled, democratic enterprise may apply in undertaking strategic planning.

Differentiating "Where" and "How"

At the simplest level, the distinction between "where" and "how" must be made clearer. (This distinction is more frequently made with "what" and "how," but *where* is more in keeping with the planning concept of direction finding.) To turn to the earliest application of that fundamental difference, consider an analogy to the early food gatherers: "Where" is *doing the right thing* by stalking animals collectively; sharpening arrows around the campfire is a "how" activity, *doing things right*. The college CEO focusing on cost containment, the government agency focusing on reporting requirements, and the firm stressing cost of production are all sharpening arrows. There is no question about the importance of sharp arrows, but concentrating on arrow sharpening leads to starvation.

A Compass as Metaphor: Pathfinding

A recent criticism of the approach of industry to strategic planning emphasizes the metaphor of a compass (Hayes 1985). The compass points direction. The environment is a swamp. The organization finds its way by determining a direction of travel through a swamp. Some writers call it pathfinding (Peters and Waterman 1982); others distinguish between the "Cook's Tour" approach to planning and the "Lewis and Clark" model:

> *The Cook's Tour defines a precise schedule on a well-defined route; it moves in an orderly progression past known landmarks. Its aim is to avoid contingencies and the unknown and to structure planning in a scheduled, ordered, and routine manner. On the other hand, the Lewis and Clark model incorporates a sense of adventure in the exploration of new planning frontiers. Lewis and Clark had a clear sense of context, direction, and what to look for, but their actual course was unknown* (Enarson 1975, quoted in Norris and Poulton 1987, p. 3).

The college deciding to emphasize community service more makes a strategic choice. That is a direction of travel. Hiring the right person to direct the continuing education program is a tactic, a step taken toward getting there.

The university hospital first carefully analyzing health needs and then services offered by competing hospitals and then choosing to emphasize short-term, emergency, and at-home, family-related services chooses a strategic market niche to occupy. Advertising its service on buses and over the radio becomes implementation. Hiring doctors and nurses with values and skills emphasizing family, emergency, and short-term care is implementation.

The short-term university president (he lasted about three years) who was immersed in issues such as the appropriate vacation allowances for various members of staff, the appropriate faculty (business or public administration) to teach general management courses, and the appropriate roles of various administrative committees was spending too much time sharpening arrows.

While the university president was sharpening arrows, one faculty group was conducting retreats that focused on mission review without considering anything occurring in its environment (Cope 1988). The issues tended to be on whether research or teaching was more important—or what research was. This faculty appeared to be oblivious to dozens of reports and articles calling for reform, the emphasis on world competitiveness, the information age, and the growing concern of the state's governor and legislature about what the tax dollar was buying. They appeared to be on a path going nowhere in particular. Or maybe they were on the wrong path: Some faculty were still adding courses focusing on developments in Europe and the sociology of American industry while Japan became the world's leading manufacture of automobiles, South Korea became a world contender in steel production and shipbuilding, and Malaysia became a leading exporter of semiconductors.

The application of the concept of "where," when articulated by the leadership and reinforced by rewards (read "budget allocations") improves the alignment of the institution's semiautonomous departments and functional units (see figure 8).

Positioning as a Major Integrating Concept
Whether the topic is planning models (Peterson 1980; Peterson et al. 1986), organizational models (Cope 1985a), systems of strategy (Chaffee 1985), strategic leadership styles (Chaffee and Tierney 1988), or some other paradigm in the jungle of organizational and management theory, it is important to identify a viable perspective or set of perspectives from which to work;

FIGURE 8

FOCUSING ON DIRECTIONS TO OBTAIN INTEGRATED EFFORT

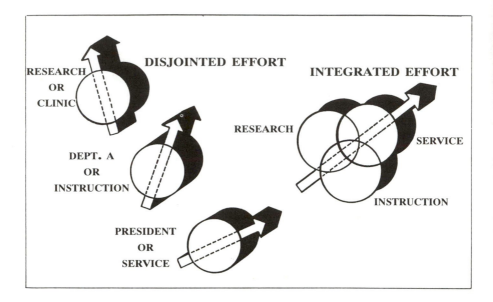

thus, positioning is frequently offered as a means to integrate thinking. Positioning is a simple, yet powerful construct.

Positioning is important in two senses. On the one hand, it is helpful to take a position, albeit tentatively, toward the theoretical constructs suggested by those who write about the strategy concept; on the other hand, positioning is advanced as an important perspective to determine what must be done relative to the environment to acquire the resources that contribute to the bottom line. An important question relative to the bottom line is easily overlooked when doing strategic planning: "How do organizations acquire resources?"

The answer, according to most business literature, is that they position themselves favorably. They find the right niche. Every enterprise exists in an environment that has technological, cultural, social, demographic, and physical properties to which it must adapt. Survival depends on resource gathering in that environment. And effective resource gathering depends on *positioning* in that environment. Colleges and universities are not exempt (Caples 1987; Trachtenberg 1985). Figure 9 illustrates positioning and niche.

Positioning in the three dimensional space illustrated by figure 9 is a matter of coalignment among needs, segments, and delivery of alternative products, technologies, prices, and places. Needs are the things people desire—from sex to security. Segments are societal groups—from embryos to those requiring hospice care. And alternatives are those programs, products, services, prices, and technologies employed to fulfill needs.

Positioning in higher education's competitive marketplace is illustrated by a marketing study of competing colleges in the Pacific Northwest in figure 10 (Leister 1975). SU, UPS, and

FIGURE 9

DEFINING POSITION ALONG THREE DIMENSIONS

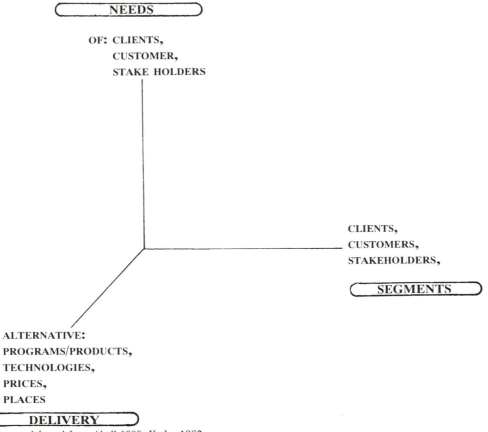

NEEDS

OF: CLIENTS,
CUSTOMER,
STAKE HOLDERS

CLIENTS,
CUSTOMERS,
STAKEHOLDERS,

SEGMENTS

ALTERNATIVE:
PROGRAMS/PRODUCTS,
TECHNOLOGIES,
PRICES,
PLACES

DELIVERY

Source: Adapted from Abell 1980; Kotler 1982.

PLU (upper right corner) are close competitors for students. The University of Washington (UW) (lower right) is almost alone; it has no local close competitors for students. With another set of variables, say adding reputation for most forms of research, UW would still stand apart from this set of competitors; however, if the "playing field" is national or international, then the competitors and means of competition change.

Using this form of analysis, a college deciding to give greater emphasis to quality, or to community service, or to lower relative pricing for tuition makes a strategic choice consistent with a direction of travel in the environment that results in a repositioning. This college has chosen a "direction of travel" to keep itself favorably positioned relative to potential resources consistent with attainment of its mission. Harvard, Bennington, Carlton, and the California Institute of Technology all maintain positions in the market. Sony and Panasonic position themselves as technology leader and technology follower. Ford positioned itself early as an international automobile firm, getting a positioning jump on GM, which Ford maintains with its Escort and Tracer. And so it is with the divisions of any enterprise. IBM competes with dozens of clones in the personal computer market and with Digital Equipment, Xerox, and a few others when it comes to large, integrated systems.

Positioning is both macro and micro: An institution's positioning is macro, its departments' positioning micro. Macro and industry *environments* parallel to macro and micro *positioning* (see later discussion).

Thus, to restate several key principles:

1. Organizations acquire all resources from their environment. And to acquire resources they seek to position themselves advantageously.
2. Planning for an enterprise is an expression of leadership in whole system design.[7]
3. Strategic planning *moves* and "strategic" management *shapes* the enterprise.

The Environment as Ecosystems
The environment may be seen as a big river of ideas and opportunities. For example, Rensselaer Polytechnic Institute (RPI)

---

7. "Whole system design" is a term taken from a master's degree program of Antioch University–Seattle.

FIGURE 10
JOINT-SPACE MAP OF INSTITUTIONAL MARKET

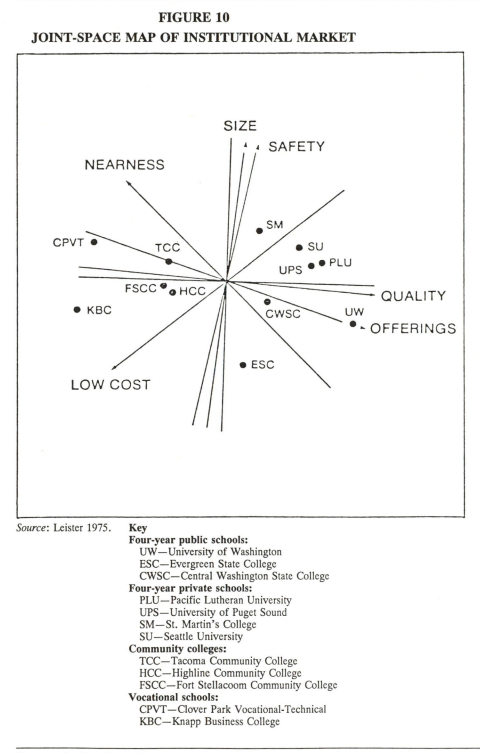

Source: Leister 1975.

Key

Four-year public schools:
UW—University of Washington
ESC—Evergreen State College
CWSC—Central Washington State College

Four-year private schools:
PLU—Pacific Lutheran University
UPS—University of Puget Sound
SM—St. Martin's College
SU—Seattle University

Community colleges:
TCC—Tacoma Community College
HCC—Highline Community College
FSCC—Fort Stellacoom Community College

Vocational schools:
CPVT—Clover Park Vocational-Technical
KBC—Knapp Business College

and Carnegie-Mellon University saw, as early as the 1970s, the opportunity in this big river of ideas to emphasize computers and information systems as integrating themes in their curricula and research.

Every college can look around and see other institutions looking into the future and moving early—reading the anticipated environment today and making today's choices. In Ohio, Hiram College moved faster than its sister Ohio Athletic Conference institutions into the adult market, while Washington state's Edmonds Community College moved fastest among community colleges into industrial training, business incubators, and Pacific-oriented, international programs (Borton 1987b). In like fashion, RPI, in the late 1970s, decentralized student recruiting and job placement to the midwest, southwest, and southeast to reposition itself to avoid the effects of the decline in high school enrollments in New York; in early 1972, RPI took a leading position regarding computer technology, indicating it would become the most computer-intensive institution in the United States. About the same time, Carnegie-Mellon University began positioning academic resources around the theme of information to unite programs as diverse as history and electrical engineering. Seattle University's School of Engineering saw the growing importance of software when the PC revolution hit in the late 1970s and began the nation's first degree program for software engineering.

The environment, that big river of ideas, is filled with opportunity, and leading institutions and businesses pay close attention to their environments and the key actors in those environments (Peters and Waterman 1982). A study of university budgeting practices points out that "to understand the behavior of an organization, you must understand the context of that behavior. Organizations are inescapably bound up with the conditions of the environment. Indeed, it has been said that all organizations engage in activities [that] have as their logical conclusion adjustment to the environment" (Pfeffer and Salancik 1978, p. 117). The truth of that observation is demonstrated in a detailed study of the connection between the organizational positioning behaviors of the University of Michigan and the Michigan legislature over two decades (Gill 1987).

Positioning in the big river is most effective when it builds on related currents. Lufthansa, for example, scanned the emerging transport environment and saw the importance of the convergence of two trends: faster delivery and smaller components. The airline became a world leader in moving freight by air by capitalizing on those trends by ordering, as early as the late 1970s, the first all cargo B-747s.

Many colleges and universities—along with firms like Sony, Phillips, and Motorola—are moving as fast as possible today to relate to the flow of an annual $200 billion in sales of telecommunications; they all see that telecommunications has a leap of about a century on the computer industry (Johnson 1984). The computer industry, the publishing industry, and the demand for offices are other main streams converging with the main stream of telecommunications. Faster and ever-faster information retrieval, word processing, and communications are demanded.

Thus, the turbulence in the big river of the computer industry is already made up of voice, picture, and data transmission. And a new tributary is the disk in a CD-ROM system, each of which will store about 250,000 pages of printed material, more than enough for a dictionary. Some leading firms and institutions are reading the environment of telecommunications and moving strategically to position themselves ahead of the competition (Borton 1987a; Johnson 1984).

Do Organizations Forget the Importance of Positioning in the Ecosystem?

Surprisingly, or so it seems, the answer is "yes." While people organize for collaborative efforts designed to achieve ends, a high proportion of resources is necessarily expended to maintain the organization itself. Sometimes, however, the pursuit of inward-looking maintenance as a means becomes an end in itself. Organizations—sometimes whole industries—appear to miss messages from "out there."

At a failing midwestern college, for example, meeting the payroll was becoming a month-to-month question, with the issue again the computer (Cope 1988). The business manager wanted it largely to keep track of costs and thus to control expenses. The director of planning wanted to use it to study market segments and successes and failures in admissions, and to integrate it into the business curriculum. The faculty just wanted it. The president did not know which way to go first.

Before the decision was made on what computer for what purpose, with the full participation of all staff, the college decided on what it saw as a two-part, turnaround strategy summarized as "maintain to gain." Part one was to contain, maintain, and reduce costs; therefore, the computer's capability was used

Every college can look around and see other institutions looking into the future and moving early— reading the anticipated environment today and making today's choices.

there first—an internal management decision. Part two was to gain; the long-run strategy was to reposition itself as a higher-quality, higher-cost institution—a plan to reposition itself in the external environment. As it was necessary to get the college's financial house in order first (while it seems contrary to the propositions of this report regarding the primacy of external choices in strategy formulation), in a case such as this one, it is appropriate to combine the internal move with the external environment and call the whole lump a "stategy." But as the results of the next two studies indicate, decisions that are dominated by internal matters do not appear conducive to long-term success.

An examination of enrollments from 1977 to 1981 at over 300 colleges in the United States found most reporting declining enrollments (Cameron and Chaffee 1983). Some were having severe difficulties with enrollments and finances; others were thriving. A targeted followup of 40 northeastern institutions reported that those deciding to concentrate on conserving resources already acquired as a basic "strategy" were less successful in gaining enrollments and less successful financially when compared to those taking initiatives in the environment (Cameron 1983). Even worse, the creative staff with the new ideas at inward-looking institutions were leaving to join institutions taking more initiatives in their environments.

Another study compared 12 institutions engaged in strategic planning with 12 matched institutions not so engaged on their comparative ability to gain resources (Meredith, Lenning, and Cope 1988). It found institutions with higher strategic scores were more successful in obtaining funds over six years (1981 through 1987) than less strategically oriented institutions. Worse, those institutions not following good strategic planning practices were actually poorer after six years. They had less money per faculty position and per student.[8]

More will be said later about the primacy of the environment, the academic enterprise's ecosystem, and how to make sense of it. Most authors take an indirect approach to considering the environment's contribution to the bottom line. Consequently, they include much more under strategies. For example, changing compensation policies, acquiring hardware and software, replacing older members of middle management, con-

8. Similar research is under way at the National Center for Postsecondary Governance and Finance as part of its Institutional Planning Project.

taining costs, and so on might all be called strategies, but they frequently do not make the distinction about the environment's being the source of *all* resources. They confuse positioning for the purpose of the acquisition of resources with every conceivable issue of management, from equipment purchases through introducing new programs to changing the nature of the college entirely. This report takes probably the narrowest conceptual view about what is really important in the long term: what the academic enterprise must do to fulfill its mission while getting the resources "out there."

Satisficing and Loose Coupling

Colleges and universities tend to be democratically governed, and control is thus neither complete nor considered desirable. As they are democracies—and given the complexity of whole system planning in changing environments and the diversity in individuals—they understand the best any institution can expect is to "satisfice." "Satisficing" is a useful term coined by Nobel Prize winner Herbert Simon to designate efforts to attain some level of satisfaction that is less than perfect. To satisfice is to do "well enough." Winston Churchill–ever the optimist–was more philosophical than his down-under cousins when reflecting on the differences between democracies and totalitarian regimes. He concluded that democracy, despite its problems, was simply the best of all possible systems. It would satisfice.

The satisficer's orientation is much like the political notion of the "art of the possible." Achieving near consensus on an institution's purposes, given the reality of divergent professional orientations (read "egos"), is possible only if the purposes are believed desirable and feasible—and if the actors share a view of what is "out there."

And given the diversity of professional orientations within most colleges and universities (even those with a reasonably well-defined mission) and the volatile possibilities in the ecosystem, it is positively desirable *not* to have—as some theorists call them—"closely coupled people or structures" (Weick 1976). The Walla Walla prison is closely coupled. Organization is tight. Control is complete.

A certain amount of loose coupling and diversification among staff and within the structures of the kinds of organizations addressed by this report should permit simultaneously divergent efforts. That diversity permits a greater possibility that the organization will innovate in response to a shifting ecosystem.

The greater danger is to a college or department with a single, possibly inappropriate purpose as the ecosystem changes.

Is the Strategic Concept Equally Useful for Any College and University?

While the comparisons that come next are overstated, they are included to make an important point: The strategic concept is not equally useful at all colleges.

Compare General Motors's strategic issues with those of Richard Vincent and Washington state's Walla Walla prison. Richard Vincent operates a 2,400-acre sheep ranch in southwest Oregon with about 1,500 sheep. General Motors, still the world's largest industrial company with annual sales of about $100 billion and over 750,000 employees, makes about 7 million automobiles annually. The Walla Walla prison restrains about 1,200 inmates.

While these groups are of different sizes, size is not important regarding what is or is not strategic. The first consideration is still the environment.

GM is a global industry that operates at 80 to 90 percent of capacity. GM can build more cars than it can sell. Vincent is also in a global industry, but he can sell as many sheep as he can produce. The Walla Walla prison is already over capacity.

GM faces two environmental issues: worldwide overcapacity and, at the time of this writing, declining interest in buying GM cars. GM is responding by slimming down production (largely an internal adjustment) and by introducing new models to escape the impression that GM cars are all made with the same cookie cutter—an external adjustment.

Because Vincent does not interact directly with the consumer of his sheep, he simply has to take the price available at the time of sale. His primary drive is to make his land productive by clearing forests, planting the right grasses, moving sheep to the right pastures, and keeping them healthy.

The prison–not so simply–finds places for those sent by the courts. Neither Vincent nor the Walla Walla prison can reposition themselves. They have no *external* strategy to consider.

GM, however, can redesign models, change prices, change locations, and decide on various promotional messages to sell GM cars. It can control the primary strategic variables: price, place, product, and promotion.

And so it is with diverse colleges and universities. The University of Michigan sets its own tuition; the University of

Washington cannot. Some legislatures limit the number of out-of-state students; others do not. Some institutions are constrained from offering new degree programs or presenting the older degree programs in new locations; others are not. Institution-to-institution and state-to-state differences (cf. Birnbaum 1983; Freed 1987; Gill 1987) are extended to a variety of organizations in figure 11.

Because an organization has control over pricing its service, its location of operation, and its program/product mix, it will find the strategy concept more useful (high applicability); that institution will have more "strategic" power and it may decide more of what to do and where to go. With little flexibility in price, location, or program, it has little opportunity to strategize; its options are more managerial and are likely to have to focus on matters of efficiency.

Different Levels of Planning
One of the deficiencies of planning in higher education has been not recognizing the need for planning at different "levels." Shirley (1983) devised a helpful typology for colleges and universities. His "four levels of strategy" recognize that planning is dealt with not only at the institutional level but also

FIGURE 11
APPLICATION OF THE STRATEGY CONCEPT TO ORGANIZATIONS

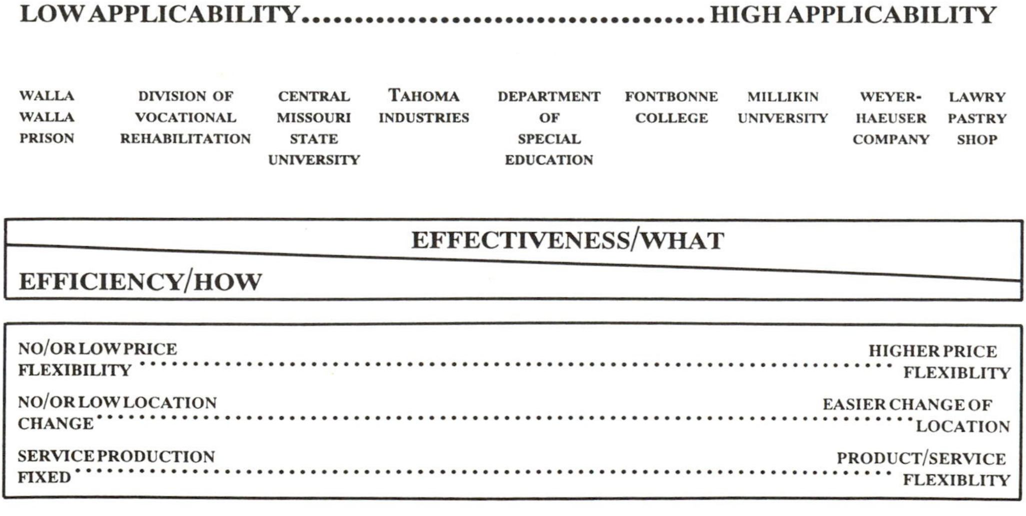

LOW APPLICABILITY.....................................HIGH APPLICABILITY

| WALLA WALLA PRISON | DIVISION OF VOCATIONAL REHABILITATION | CENTRAL MISSOURI STATE UNIVERSITY | TAHOMA INDUSTRIES | DEPARTMENT OF SPECIAL EDUCATION | FONTBONNE COLLEGE | MILLIKIN UNIVERSITY | WEYER- HAEUSER COMPANY | LAWRY PASTRY SHOP |

| EFFECTIVENESS/WHAT |
| EFFICIENCY/HOW |

| NO/OR LOW PRICE FLEXIBILITY · HIGHER PRICE FLEXIBLITY |
| NO/OR LOW LOCATION CHANGE · EASIER CHANGE OF LOCATION |
| SERVICE PRODUCTION FIXED · PRODUCT/SERVICE FLEXIBLITY |

by colleges, departments, and other functional units. The system level was added later (Pailthorp 1986).

Perhaps Shirley too overworks the term "strategy" by not differentiating between strategizing and planning and by not differentiating between what the institution cannot control and therefore must strategize about and what it does control and can reshape through planning—the strategic concept central to this report. Nevertheless, his levels include: (1) *institutional strategy*, which deals with matching environmental opportunities with internal strengths to determine clientele, goals, program mix, geographic domains, and comparative advantage; (2) *campuswide functional strategies*, which deal with the specifics of finances, human resources, enrollment, and facilities to achieve the strategies defined in level 1; (3) *program strategies*, which are academic department plans made in response to plans at levels 1 and 2; and (4) *program-level function strategies*, which are the specific plans for admissions, curriculum, staffing, and budget made by *departments* to translate strategy into operations.

Is Strategic Planning an Expression of a Different, Special Form of Leadership?

"Planning is something we do in advance of taking action; that is, it is *anticipatory decision making*. It is a process of deciding . . . before action is required" (Ackoff 1970, p. 2).

This observation is a simple one. Many examples of strategic planning and of comprehensive, master or long-range planning are filled, however, with "decisions" already made on all manner of details. These misdirected planning efforts often involve staff in activities taking many months, not uncommonly 12 or 18. The result is often a document of about 120 pages already filled with decisions for the next five or ten years. Planning documents of this size appear to be assumed magic— like a term paper of 30 pages.

The reasons the 120-page document is mistaken are, first, that future conditions for organizations in turbulent environments cannot be known and, second, future states require *sets* of interdependent decisions made in response to the changing environment. To illustrate the significance of the complexity of interdependent decisions *in a stable environment*, for example, consider planning a house, where a decision to place the living room in a particular corner has an effect on the location of every other room and hence on the "performance" of the house as a whole (Ackoff 1970).

Add a changing environment to the design of the house. The angle of the sun changes. The sun begins to rise in the west, or the south. The angle of the land shifts. The prevailing winds shift. The climate changes to more rain, or less sun, or sleet instead of snow. The placement of rooms, window blinds, drainage, house plants, windows, and so forth must be adjusted to the changed context. This is the reality of organizations in turbulent environments.

While this report, mirroring as it does trends in the current management literature, emphasizes the collaborative/participative forms of campus decision making, it does not deny the importance of leaders' anticipating the future. All levels of our college have a place for executive leadership.

Robert McHale, for example, is president of California's DeAnza Community College. DeAnza is frequently identified as one of the outstanding colleges of its type in the United States. It plans strategically. McHale keeps the college on course by providing a style of planner leadership. He borrows from the scriptures when he says to his staff, "The planners shall inherit the college budget."

The application of the concept draws on many concepts of planning and organizational behavior. Given the whole system view of strategy, an eclectic approach to process and techniques is suggested. Particularly useful ideas include (1) the importance of separating externally directed decisions (strategizing) from internally directed decisions (management), (2) recognizing that comprehensive strategizing and planning take place in at least four organizational levels, and (3) noting the limitations inherent in loosely coupled institutions that have varying capacities to plan strategically.

The next two sections are about the environment and about information. Together they are about strategic thinking, which is itself about how individuals scan environments, gather and display information, and make choices. "Strategic issues arise from the flow of information for analysis, design, and action" (Schwartz 1987, p. 4).

ENVIRONMENTAL CONTEXT: The Big Picture

Peter O'Toole, the eccentric academic in the film *Creator*, advises a student to sign up for 12 credits in the "Big Picture." This section is about the environment, the society, the ecosystem, and how institutions appear to make sense of the "Big Picture." It is about planning in two contexts: internal and external. The task in the challenge in the Big Picture is to create awareness and knowledge with scanning techniques like those illustrated for joint-problem solving.

Institutions of higher education can no longer be clearly differentiated from their environment.

Isn't the importance and significance of the environment— this total of circumstances affecting institutions of higher education—self-evident? I believe it is not. Colleges once were fairly insulated institutions, and the period of collegiate education was sharply set off from the secondary education that preceded it and the work life that followed it. This is no longer true. Neither institutions of higher education nor the experiences of their students are as sharply marked off from the "outside world" as they used to be (Jonsen 1986, p. 5).

This growing awareness of the outside environment is the single most important contribution of strategic planning to institutional decision making.

The outward-looking character of strategic planning takes into account a growing awareness and significance of the outside environment (Keller 1983). This growing awareness of the outside environment is the single most important contribution of strategic planning to institutional decision making, and three-quarters of all change at most institutions is "now triggered by outside factors" (p. 145).

Business firms and higher education look at the term "environment" differently, it should be noted. In higher education, "environment" usually conjures up the climate or culture within the institution; in business firms, the same term nearly always means what is "out there." This section is about what is "out there."

Environmental Scanning

The literature on strategy refers to environmental scanning, sometimes futures research, as a set of techniques to determine what is out there. Techniques for examining the future range from passive scanning to Monte Carlo and Trend Impact Analysis (Morrison, Renfro, and Boucher 1984). Passive scanning is what we all do everyday. We scan continually. "Passive scanning has traditionally been a major source of information about the external world for most decision makers and hence for their organizations" (p. 19).

Monte Carlo and various techniques of Trend Impact Analysis are probablistic forecasting techniques requiring quantitative manipulations of substantial complexity. Mid-range techniques for environmental scanning include variations of the Delphi technique and cross-impact analyses (Cope 1978, 1986; Morrison and Cope 1985). The application of any of these techniques should result in two outcomes: first, a greater awareness and knowledge about what is likely to happen and, second, a growing consensus about how the institution should respond.

This section describes the passive to mid-range techniques for scanning already in use.

Sources of Information

Changes in the environment are difficult to follow or anticipate. Interest, for example, in the drug culture was high in the early 1970s, nearly disappeared by the end of the 1970s, and is peaking again as this report is written. So it is with other matters—aging, energy, sexism, insurance coverage, nuclear waste, education, medical care, and tax reform. Groups doing an environmental scan therefore need to be aware of the difference between a cycle and a trend. A shift in interest (a cycle) changes faster than basic problems or opportunities.

Many sources of information are available (see, for example, Ahumada and Hefferlin 1986; Halstead 1987, 1988; Morrison 1987). The *Higher Education Bibliographic Yearbook*, for example, provides up-to-date information on what is currently the best literature in the 34 topic areas summarized by teams of experts on higher education.[9]

9. They include teaching and learning; curriculum; faculty; libraries; graduate education, research, and public service; student characteristics and development; recruitment, admissions, and retention; student affairs and services; institutional mission, quality, and accreditation; governance and the presidency; institutional and academic management; institutional advancement; institutional financing and budgeting; business and personnel administration; institutional planning and research; academic and institutional computing and communications; campus and building planning and management; national and federal policy; national system comparisons and development; statewide planning and coordination; finance and resource allocation; assessment, evaluation, and outcomes analysis; educational opportunity; student financial assistance; work, education, and industry; history; philosophy; law; economics; sociology, anthropology, demography; independent higher education; community colleges; private career schools; and adult and continuing education.

Another source of expert information comes from centers for assessing environmental trends or specific events, such as the center that existed from 1985 to 1987 at the University of Southern California. To help organizations anticipate events, the School of Business Administration at the university established the Club of 1000 in 1985. One thousand experts continually assessed information and provided opinions to the Center for Futures Research on the likely developments in 45 areas, from agricultural biology to welfare. Analyses of the results of the expert assessments of the future make it obvious that "expert" knowledge comes largely from the popular literature, which—watch out—might be quite wrong.

For example, in response to a question in 1985 about the possibility that Mexican oil reserves could prove to be as vast as those in Saudi Arabia, 53 percent of the respondents identified their source for knowing this fact was the popular literature, 4 percent claimed first-hand knowledge, 33 percent knew from professional literature, and 10 percent knew it was likely from some form of oral communication.

Only in the narrow matters, such as the likelihood that sophisticated software could be developed capable of creating its own computer programs to solve complex analytic problems, were respondents more likely to form their opinions from first-hand knowledge plus professional literature (81 percent); only 8 percent of respondents knew it from the popular literature and 11 percent knew it from some form of oral communication. The popular literature was identified as the prime source, or was at least as good as any other source, in 151 out of 197 events.

Thus, it seems, if we can rely on the experts on our campuses and on the popular literature, little needs to be added to the current fund of knowledge among knowledgeable people who are actively, although passively, scanning the environment all the time. In most of the cases of strategic planning illustrated earlier, little attention was given to specialized data gathering. More will be said in the next section on information about the limited data necessary for making strategic choices.

Mid-Range Models for Environmental Scanning

One purpose of this section is to point out what is not so obvious about what we call "the environmental context," to demonstrate why that environmental context is frequently underexplored and that it operates on at least two levels: mega and industry.

Professionals are all scanning passively nearly all the time. The process is at play when we read the Sunday paper or the morning edition of the daily paper; it is at play when we listen to the hourly newscasts, watch documentaries, read government reports, and attend professional meetings. We constantly make personal forecasts.

Individuals as Storehouses of Information

Individually, each student, faculty member, administrator, and so on, is a warehouse of information. To tap the wealth of existing information, resourcefulness, and creativity among professional staff, only a little structure is necessary (Cope 1988; Morrison and Cope 1985; Morrison, Renfro, and Boucher 1984). One simple structure is STEP: systematically review Sociodemographic changes, then Technology changes, then Economic changes, and finally Political changes (Cope 1988; Jonsen 1986; Morrison, Renfro, and Boucher 1984; Wilson 1974). STEP is built into the next, more complete environmental scanning model.

STEP/SOS System

A more complex—possibly more complete—approach to scanning is illustrated in figure 12, a simple device to help a group explore what it already knows. It is called the Braudel-Wilson system, or the STEP/SOS system.

Fernand Braudel was a European historian who wrote a famous history of the Mediterranean during the Age of Philip the II (1556–98). Ian Wilson is a management consultant–futurist with the Stanford Research Institute.

Braudel, in preparing his history of the Mediterranean, discovered history occurred on three concurrent levels: (1) the day-to-day developments read in the morning papyrus scrolls in Rome; (2) the larger structural changes occurring as, for example, when Venice grew and then declined as a commercial power; and (3) individual opinions, attitudes, beliefs, and values.

"These three levels of history can also serve as a means for viewing the future" (Morrison, Renfro, and Boucher 1984, p. 5). Most forecasting is based upon surface changes, such as changes in employment, rates of inflation, sales of houses, housing starts, and sales of automobiles. They are the matters on the front page of the daily newspaper or reported in the *Chronicle of Higher Education*. This level of analysis is inadequate, however,

FIGURE 12

STEP/SOS ENVIRONMENT
ASSESSMENT MODEL

because underlying shifts of longer-term significance are not sought. The result has been the surprise development that upsets the long-term trend analysis based on surface indicators.

For example, at the surface of education in today's newspapers are endless reports of inadequacies among graduates who cannot read or write or who do not know the facts of geography. At the same time is occurring an underlying—and therefore more important—trend in industry: The percentage of nonjudgmental, routine jobs is declining rapidly. The long-term result will be an increased demand among graduates to know how to think and how to make judgments in a global economy.

A second level is to look for the implications of structural/institutional changes, such as the shift from factory-based to office-based employment, the movement of post-WWII babies through the decades, and the shift of the center of economic activity from the Atlantic to the Pacific Basin. They are the megatrends.

The third level of analysis (again from Braudel's formulation) is the process of exploring the value changes occurring over time. For example, data gathered annually by the Cooperative Institutional Research Program at UCLA have illustrated that freshmen college students are changing their life expectations. During 1967, over 80 percent of the freshmen entering colleges across the United States wanted, during college years, to "develop a meaningful philosophy of life." By the late 1980s, that proportion had shifted to less than 50 percent. In 1967, fewer than 50 percent emphasized "being well off financially," but in recent years, that criterion became important to over 70 percent.

Braudel looked backward to learn how to interpret the present and the future. Wilson looks forward from the present.

Ian Wilson was a leading administrator in the nation's early programs of exploration in space and a pioneer of sociopolitical forecasting. He suggests the value of looking for trends in four arenas: political, sociodemographic, economic, and technological (1974).[10] Figure 13 shows a conceptual representation of environmental cross impacts.

10. Jonsen (1986), writing about the environmental context of higher education, applies approximately the same system: demographic, economic, political, technical, social, and organizational environments. (The usual breakdown of external forces combines social and demographic.) Because organizational is internal, even Jonsen's scheme follows the usual *four* cross impacts (economic, social, technical, and political).

FIGURE 13
CONCEPTUAL REPRESENTATION OF ENVIRONMENTAL CROSS IMPACTS

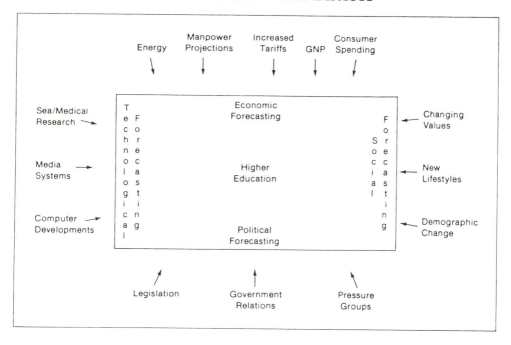

Wilson's arenas can be remembered by the acronym STEP: socio-demographic, technological, economic, and political. Braudel's levels become SOS: superficial or surface (day-to-day) events, opinions (more deeply held values and beliefs), and structures (major shifts in organizations or society). Together STEP and SOS summarize forces working in the environment that suggest contextual opportunities and warn of threats.

It seems clear that forces operating within any of Braudel's levels or Wilson's arenas are probably recursive. That is, a technological breakthrough in an arena, such as the birth control pill, can be seen as either a cause or a result of changed attitudes toward sexual values, the dynamics of the baby boom, the need for two-worker households, emerging personal roles for men and women, and so on.

Braudel argued that a change in any level could cause a change in another level. A change could be "initiated" in any level, causing changes in the other levels. For example, the

FIGURE 14
GENERAL SCHEME FOR ENVIRONMENTAL SCANNING

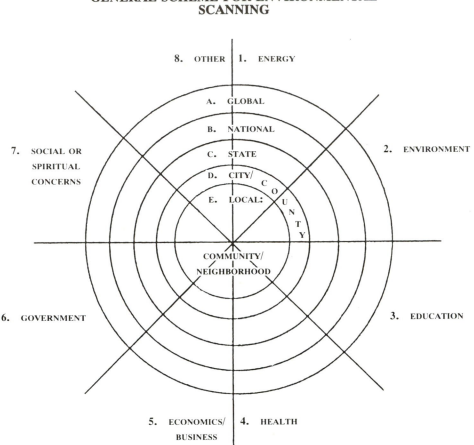

surface occurrence of seeing more beggars on the streets of the once-prosperous, smaller Roman or Greek towns during the middle period of the Roman Empire's prosperity was "initiated" (Braudel's term) by the trade monopoly and increased use of slaves in a few dominant city-states like Venice or Florence. At the same time, a surface change was the noisy procession honoring newer gods, such as Dionysus or Bacchus, gods of wine and life, while an underlying decline occurred in morals.

Completing the model—like filling the squares of a crossword puzzle—that interweaves Braudel's levels with Wilson's four domains is a useful device for informing judgment about

FIGURE 15
EXAMPLE OF STEP IN AN ENVIRONMENTAL
SCANNING MODEL

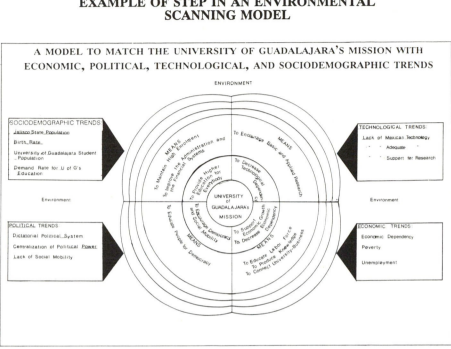

A MODEL TO MATCH THE UNIVERSITY OF GUADALAJARA'S MISSION WITH
ECONOMIC, POLITICAL, TECHNOLOGICAL, AND SOCIODEMOGRAPHIC TRENDS

Source: Romeromorett and Riveravargas. 1987.

what is really happening "out there." Members of a planning committee can be asked to think through an environmental scan with an enlarged form of figure 12, perhaps on legal size paper. Then they can compare what they filled in to start the analysis.

Other Devices for Environment Scanning
The general scheme in figure 14 is also useful for registering or noting changes occurring "out there." Again members of a planning committee can fill in the spaces and make comparisons starting with what is occurring locally and extending observations outward to global observations. The categories are arbitrary for this illustration. Note, for example, it includes no arena for technology. The general schematic should be adapted for a given institution; categories can be added or subtracted as appropriate.

Figure 15, developed as part of the preparation for a strategic analysis at the University of Guadalajara, Mexico, is a mega-level of analysis useful to develop the fullest contextual perspective among those who will participate in the institution's policy choices. It is an actual example of the general scheme shown in figure 14, modified with STEP from figure 13. Note that the institution is at the center, including dimensions of its mission (ends and means), relating in the quadrants to the sociodemographic, technological, economic, and political environments.

More detailed assessments of the trends, for example, in the technology quadrant (upper right) would lead to a sense of the priority to give the "means" identified in the economics quadrant (lower right). One of this illustration's more desired features is the presentation of the institution in its largest context on one page. The actual analysis for this institution was supported by maps of Guadalajara (the city), Jalisco (the state), and the adjacent regions of Mexico. In addition, the presentation included a substantial body of demographic information (on the single page) beyond the detail already shown in the upper left quadrant.

INFORMATION IN CONTEXT: Minds Perceiving

This section is about bits of data and individual minds processing information.

Harlan Cleveland, formerly president of the University of Hawaii, now director of the Humphrey Institute at the University of Minnesota, and author of *The Knowledge Executive* (1985a), says some provocative things about knowing, information, and knowledge. In discussing leadership, he says, "Your responsibility increases in direct ratio to your ignorance." He calls attention to executives who, as they move up the ladder in a complex, ever-changing world, manage more while understanding less. He also observes, "The obvious escape from this dilemma is not to learn more about the details of whatever-it-is but to learn more about its *context*" (p. xvi).

The premise of Cleveland's book is that the progress of science and technology, driven by the fusion of computers and telecommunications, is changing the world for those who get things done by leading others. Each has to "graduate from the mind-set of an expert to organize his or her mind for the analysis and projection of breadth" (p. xvii).

That our society is becoming an information society is now a cliché. Information is at the heart of the decision process. Information is the substance of communication. Communication is the substance of leadership. Strategic thinking is a matter of information processing. Strategic leadership is helping all those who will do the strategic thinking learn about context (cf. above).

This section progresses from summarizing the more traditional ways information has been conceived of to the more recent ways of looking at information. In summary, the more traditional tended to look at information as information in bits, categorized by form, and by the ways it was applied. The usual references were to management information systems or decision support systems.

More recent views have placed *knowledge* (as derived from information) in a larger context of how the mind perceives and processes information and how information in varying forms is used to create a vision and communicated to influence. "Knowledge has become inseparable from power in modern society" (Rolf 1987, p. 2).

Information and Organizational Purpose

With the widespread introduction of organizational theory and strategic/contextual management concepts into enterprises dur-

Communication is the substance of leadership.

---

ing the 1970s, the need for an additional perspective on information requirements became evident (Peterson et al. 1986). The technically oriented information requirements of the sixties and early seventies were being supplemented by "managerially oriented" systems. It became clear that the information for strategic purposes available to institutions is less costly, simpler, and can be more directly related to the long-term success of the institution (Baker 1982; Carroll et al. 1984; Cope 1986; Rockart 1982; Sapp 1985; Sullivan 1985).

The current introduction of the contextual/strategic planning concepts requires a new approach to information. The "technically oriented" information requirements of the seventies and early eighties needs supplementation by strategically oriented systems. Most information systems, whether computerized or not, were designed for operating and control purposes and provide internal, historical information, whereas strategic choices require information frequently in the form of intelligence about future, external conditions.

Cope (1986) following Ohmae (1983) has proposed a strategic triangle concept (see figure 16) for systematic information gathering for making two types of sequenced decisions: first for strategic choices and then for shaping, resource allocation and control (cf. figure 1). Key success factors help discriminate further the information required at each vertex of the triangle (Sullivan 1985).

FIGURE 16
THE STRATEGIC INFORMATION TRIANGLE

INSTITUTION

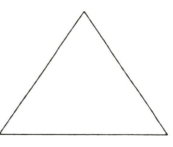

STAKE HOLDERS   COMPETITION

The Strategic Triangle for Information

The triangle concept is deceptively simple. Reduced to its essentials, effective strategy deals with the interplay of institution, competition, and stake holders.

- *Stake holders* are students, government agencies, foundations, communities, and so on. Any entity having a particular interest in the "products" of the institution becomes a stake holder (Mitroff 1983).
- *Stake holder's information* must include (or so it seems) trend analyses on application rates, admitted students, indices of students' quality, retention-to-graduation ratios, changing characteristics over time, and so on. Additional information—depending on the institution—would include new initiatives in government-sponsored research, changing initiatives of foundations, the attitudes of alumni, and so on.
- *Competitors' information* is about competing institutions on matters such as faculty salaries and benefits, levels of student financial aid offered, new program ventures, accreditation reviews, tuition levels, and so on. It is clear that the least developed and potentially most valuable set of information that is not developed at most institutions concerns its competition.
- *Institutional information* must include indices of program quality, market viability, faculty turnover, costs, and so on.

Key Success Factors and Key Success Indicators

Key success factors (KSFs) are those few key choices around which favorable results are necessary: secure the local market; move to the upper third in tuition levels, retain a lively curriculum. Information systems should develop key success indicators (KSIs) to assess progress on a KSF. For example, the college intending to increase its tuition needs to track annually the competition's tuition charges. KSIs are necessary to assess progress along the direction of travel relative to the external environment.

In addition, some KSIs at each point of the triangle are universally important (student numbers and quality, for example). Other KSIs will differ, however, depending on the strategic choices already made. (It may be useful to look again at figure

1.) When Rensselaer Polytechnic, for example, decided to broaden its base of recruitment, declining proportions of students from its traditional areas was an indication of success. As the private liberal arts college in that midwestern city (mentioned earlier) decided to move its tuition level from the bottom third into the top third of the institutions in its zones of competition, relatively lower tuitions charged among competing institutions was an indication of success. When the University of Michigan decided to shift millions of dollars out of some colleges over five years to other uses, the changing ratios were signs that certain goals were being achieved. (Note, however, that the Michigan example may not have been for strategic objectives; that is, objectives may not have been directly associated with the external environment.)

The triangle concept of information about KSFs and KSIs implies that a successful strategy must be defined as an endeavor by the institution to differentiate itself in the larger marketplace positively from its competition—on those three dimensions. A strategic move changes the institution, its stake holders, *and* its competition. Anything less is not strategic, only tactical, as in the example of the University of Michigan above.

When RPI announced—over 10 years ago—that it would become the most computerized American university in the country, initiated recruiting and job placement in selected locations in other parts of the country, and developed new contractual relationships with startup, high-technology businesses, it changed the *institution*, it developed new communities of *stake holders*, and it differentiated itself further from *competing* institutions. These moves were clearly strategic, based upon strategic choices. Each institution should develop its own KSFs and KSIs, depending upon its distinctive strategy (Cope 1986).

Information Follows Purpose
The strategic planning process, the strategic plans made (choices), and the resulting strategic management (controls, structures, rewards, and so on) require far less information than is commonly available and need it selectively, infrequently, in aggregated form, and with low accuracy. Table 3 contrasts characteristics of useful information across three purposes, from operational to strategic.

For further understanding and the eventual design of distinc-

TABLE 3
CHARACTERISTICS OF INFORMATION AND INSTITUTIONAL PURPOSE

Characteristic	Purpose		
	Strategic planning	*Tactical planning management control, and guidance*	*Operational control*
Time horizon	Present and future		Past and present
Source of information	External		Internal
Type of information	Qualitative		Quantitative
Level of detail	Aggregate		Detailed
Accuracy	Low		High
Range of variables	Wide		Narrow
Frequency of use	Infrequent		Frequent
Currency of information	Low		High

Source: Arns and Curran 1982.

tive institution-based and academic unit–based information requirements, some additional distinctions from the traditional
perspectives on the uses of information are useful. *Data* or *da-
tum* is understood to mean a single element or a fact. *Information* is an aggregate of data so used as to become knowledge.
"Data" has no intrinsic significance until it becomes information, and information itself is meaningless until related to some
purpose. The information that is the subject of this report is
seen to serve three institutional purposes: operations, control,
and strategy. The emphasis, however, is on the strategic planning purpose, as that is where the deficiency is greatest (Heydinger 1983), because college and university planning itself has
developed through four stages (Heydinger 1983): Budget Planning (1) to Goals and Objectives Planning (2) to Forecasting
(3) to Strategic (4). As each form of planning was adopted, appropriate supporting information systems developed.

Operational information is maintained on a day-to-day basis
to record and ensure performance; it is a highly accurate and
detailed record of the past and present about students, expendi-
tures, facilities, and so on. It has almost no strategic value. It
is gathered as unfocused by-products of operating system requirements. Reports from the operating system are essentially
spin-offs from a system designed to perform routine, bottom-

up, paperwork processing. Too much emphasis is still placed on this mind-narrowing information among offices of institutional research.

Information for the purpose of guidance and *control* involves year-to-year tactical decisions about the deployment of resources and their effective and efficient application. *Information for strategic purposes* aids in the delineation of alternative courses of direction that have time horizons three to ten years away. Operational information is for maintenance, information for control is for managing and guiding the institution, and information for strategic purposes is for adjusting new situations. Adjusting to new situations requires the selective gathering of data and converting those data to information, subsequently to knowledge, and ultimately to sound strategic choices.

Computers or Intelligence

Much strategic information is in the form of unstructured "intelligence." Intelligence is future oriented, quickly assembled, subjective, often delivered word of mouth from creditable sources. The strongest advocates of the need for intelligence may conclude that all computer-based reports will be useless for strategy. Table 4 shows the relationship between the types of decisions and decision-supporting information systems suggested here.

TABLE 4
EXAMPLES OF TYPES OF DECISIONS AND
DECISION-SUPPORTING INFORMATION SYSTEMS

	Operations	Management	Strategic
Structured	Billing students Registrar's records	Admission of students Class registration	Mix of students
Semistructured	Class scheduling Inventory control	Cost analysis Fund management	Location of functions
	Computer Useful		
Unstructured	Installation of PERT	New equipment or marketing effort	New degree programs

Table 4 is an extension of the concept presented in Table 3. Here, the information required depends on both the purpose (operations to strategic) and the degree of regularity (structure in the institution). The most important decisions for change are unstructured and relate most closely to features of the environment.

As decisions are less structured, less routine, less frequent, and move away from operating tasks, the need for environmental scanning, intelligence, and the application of wisdom in decision making increases.

In summary, data and information systems are usually developed from transactions in functional units (admissions, accounts payable, and so on) and provide information bottom up. By beginning with KSF strategies and ideas about indicators of successful movement KSI's, one reverses the process by which institutions develop information systems.

The job of supplementing existing data and information systems is not as large as it may seem, because only a limited number of key variables are available to capture. Some are temporal, key for a time. The list of factors differs from institution to institution and from strategic academic unit to unit, from one set of personal preferences to another set of personal preferences.

At least three benefits accrue that may not be so obvious for developing sets of information following the strategic triangle concept with its related KSIs:

1. Managers, chairs, presidents, deans, and so on, are clearer about those factors requiring attention. The process of determining strategy and KSFs and KSIs ensures that significant factors receive scrutiny.
2. Identifying KSFs and KSIs allows for a limited definition of the amount of information that must be collected regularly.
3. Acknowledging the temporal nature of the information requirements put the information system in constant flux, with new formats of reports accompanying new ways of thinking about strategic choices.

Most information systems already in place in our institutions, whether computerized or not, have been designed for *operations* (paying bills and collecting funds, for example) and *control* (meeting the requirements of government agencies, determining unit costs, for example). This information provides essential internal, historical information. The information important to the leadership role identified throughout this report (strategic choices, making sense of purpose) requires data, facts, information, knowledge, even rumors obtained through intelligence—all leading to tacit understanding or wisdom.

The synthesis sought may be in Cleveland's thinking from *The Knowledge Executive* (1985a). Regardless of the type of organization, he identifies a hierarchical system starting with data, then information, then knowledge, and finally wisdom. Strategic plans he places at his level of wisdom. He is concerned that wisdom will be lost in the search for more data, more information, and more knowledge.

Information is horizontal, knowledge is structured and hierarchical, wisdom is organismic and flexible. Any diligent student can, with the help of a computerized system, acquire vast amounts of information—for instance, the population of every township in the United States. But the data are pretty useless because they are stretched out at one level. (Information is horizontal.) For the data to be useful—come to life, as it were—they have to be linked to another rung or category of data. The result is knowledge. (Knowledge is structured and hierarchical.) Every teacher knows how difficult it is to pass knowledge, as distinct from information, to students; hence, we give objective tests to determine how much information, rather than knowledge, they have acquired. As for imparting wisdom, it has much to do with personal chemistry and slow osmosis (Yi-fu Tuan, quoted in Cleveland 1985a, p. 23).

Visual knowledge sharing (as illustrated in the case examples) may be the most powerful means to convey meaning. Through visual cues constructed by the participants, they may have been better able to see into the experience of others. The visual representations mixed together, in almost random streams of realities, out of which strategic sense making was possible.

Nobel Prize winner Czelaw Milosz says of this largely unverbalized territory:

The human imagination is spatial and it is constantly constructing an architectonic whole from landscapes remembered or imagined; it progresses from what is closest to what is farther away, winding layers or strands round the single axis, which begins where the feet touch the ground (quoted in Cleveland 1985a, p 7).

If all this sounds fanciful, consider that the University of Pennsylvania's seminars on strategic management and leadership teach planning using managers' drawings of firms. Senior executives from business firms draw pictures. The seminar's director says the exercise forces the participants to think of their company as a whole. "The drawings express the holistic sense of where the company is and where it is going" (Davis 1984).

Researchers at the University of Washington are studying how individuals, from the mentally handicapped to intellectually gifted graduate students, process images containing both words and pictures. They test the use of graphics and maps on retention of knowledge in what they call a "chunking strategy" (remembering clusters of elements in groups). Their research, like that of Nobel laureate Herbert Simon, blends the verbal and visual, the linear and intuitive, the cognitive and affective intellectual powers in ways still little understood except as tacit knowledge (Rolf 1987).

Insofar as whole system planning is a shaping process akin to the spatial demands of pottery, architecture, and design, it is useful to know planning research among those planning buildings and urban settings acknowledge that among the six or more senses, the visual is the most important (Porteous 1982). We may be more influenced by pictures, charts, and stories than by data sets. Pictures and stories are whole and "real," data abstract. Several of the case examples presented earlier demonstrate contextual planning with pictures. Visualizing is thought to be especially compatible with the strategic concept; that is why this report uses a substantial number of illustrations.

Visualization Leads to Synthesizing
Visual cues are multidimensional. Because the cues are multidimensional, synthesizing is more complete and the synthesis has more depth—it has integration. Visual presentations evolve from hind*sight*, therefore capturing the traditions of the organization. A world *view* provides for seeing and interpreting new developments and trends in the largest geographic perspective. Depth *perception* is enhanced if factors are illustrated in appropriate detail. The responses of other competing or collaborative

organizations or other stake holders is taken into consideration by providing *peripheral vision.*

Vision itself, of course, is essentially *foresight.* It is the culmination, the pulling together of hindsight, the world view, peripheral vision, and depth perception. Finally, the contextual process leads to re-*vision.* Revision changes past strategy and revises, continually, institutional strategy as environmental changes are re-*viewed.*

The Mind

Furthermore, it is contended, only the properly prepared human mind, operating at milliseconds, is able to assemble the variety of views necessary for strategic choice making. Only the human brain has the transcending ability to integrate so many signals, images, and forecasts and select from among alternative actions. Only the mind can get into the space beyond ordinary planning to assemble images that are at once clear and energizing.

Only the mind is capable of constructing word pictures in the form of metaphor that captures the *emotional* and intellectual rightness of what is to come: the vision.

> *When the problems to be solved are more than trivial, the recognition processes have to be organized in a coherent way and they must be supplied with reasoning capabilities that allow inferences to be drawn from the information retrieved, and the numerous chunks of information combined. Hence, intuition is not a process that operates independently of analysis; rather, the two processes are essential complementary components of effective decision-making systems* (Simon 1987, p. 61).

Right-Brained and Left-Brained Thinking

Aristotle concluded the heart was where humans did their thinking. The brain was simply little more than a "radiator," something simply to cool the blood. Twenty-two hundred years later, in our era of brain surgery and heart transplants, it may be amusing to think of Aristotle's miscalculations, but much remains to be learned about the brain.

The literature on conceptualizing has been dominated by speculations on brain hemispheres. One side is associated with logic, order, reason, linear thinking, mathematics, the other with art, feeling, openness, subjectivity, and imagery. C.P. Snow, in *Two Cultures and the Scientific Revolution,* hypothesized the existence of two cultures, the scientists and the humanists.

A synergistic alliance must result between the logical and intuitive sides of our dispositions, and the same synergistic alliance must exist among our colleagues who exhibit both tendencies. It is, however, "the generalists, for better or worse, who box the compass, chart the course, and say where we shall go together" (Cleveland 1985a, p. 47). So it is the perspective of the generalist the strategic concept seeks, whatever our skills.

FOUNDATIONS OF THE STRATEGIC CONCEPT

Because it has been claimed in this report and elsewhere (Gray 1986; Hayes 1986) that both conceptual and pragmatic confusion has blunted the potential value of the strategic concept, this section explores the foundation providing intellectual substance. It is written more for the student of the strategic concept than for the administrator.

Much of the existing confusion results because few of those who advocate or claim they are using the strategic concept understand its foundations. They do anything and modify it with the term "strategic." But there is an important distinction: "Strategic issues are those that deal with the organization's relationship with the environment and affect most of the organization. Thus, all strategic issues are important, but not all important issues are strategic" (Norris and Poulton 1987, p. 14).

Although the distinctions found among the following foundations are not always operationally clear, it will be helpful to the planner and researcher to be aware of the foundations to make appropriate adaptations in practice and in research.

The literature appears to offer at least four foundations for understanding current practices and approaches to research: (1) historical-intellectual origins (Cope 1981, 1985b); (2) general management practices (Ansoff 1965, 1969, 1979, 1984; Chandler 1962); (3) planning models (Peterson 1980); and (4) organizational theory (Cope 1985a, Peterson et al. 1986).

Leadership is woven within each foundation but addressed separately by insightful writers about organizations in general (Bennis and Nanus 1985; Cleveland 1985b; Drucker 1974) or higher education institutions in particular (Chaffee and Tierney 1988; Guskin and Bassis 1986; Kauffman 1984; Kerr 1982).

Historical-Intellectual Origins and General Management Practices

It is frequently assumed but not true that the strategic planning concept began in 1962 with the publication of Alfred Chandler's *Strategy and Structure: Chapters in the History of the American Industrial Enterprise.* That book summarized the history and expansion of 100 of the nation's largest firms during the previous 100 years. Seen as the first scholarly work demonstrating that firms prosper more as they anticipate opportunity in future environments, the book built on the relations between economic and business history.

No doubt Chandler's book is of great importance, as it advanced the proposition that a firm's success results from how

Much of the existing confusion results because few of those who advocate or claim they are using the strategic concept understand its foundations.

well it reads the environment. Some firms are more responsive to the environment than others. Some firms make better strategic decisions.

The next seminal work in the general management literature was Igor Ansoff's *Corporate Strategy* (1965). Ansoff recognized three classes of decisions: strategic, administrative, and operating, each related to different aspects of converting resources. Strategic decisions, Ansoff pointed out, are concerned primarily with *external* rather than internal processes, such as what to produce for what markets. Administrative decisions emphasize *internal* hierarchical and structural dimensions, while operating decisions maximize the profitability of current operations. Most of what is written today in the business literature is similar to what was Ansoff espoused in 1965 (cf. Ansoff 1969, 1979, 1984).

Thus, Corporate Strategy *has been a forerunner in the field of strategic management. It was the first serious attempt to synthesize and unify business problems into an overall analytic approach to solving the total strategic problem of the firm.* (Toftoy 1987, p. 49).

Today's definitions and applications of strategy come largely from business school authors like Chandler and Ansoff (Chaffee 1985), but those authors and business school strategy courses seldom acknowledge an intellectual debt to far earlier geopolitical theories or to more recent general systems theories (Cope 1981, 1985b). Geopolitical-military theory extends back at least to Sun Zi, a Chinese general who wrote about the art of warfare 2,500 years ago on bamboo sticks (Cope 1985b).

More recent geopolitical-military concepts have been advanced (Mackinder 1904; Mahan 1890). Mahan's most celebrated work, *The Influence of Sea Power on History, 1660–1783,* traces the growth of maritime powers during the 17th and 18th centuries and offers six propositions for nations to achieve economic power relating to geographic positioning, form of government, the deployment of resources, and the attitudes of people and government.

Mackinder, a British geographer, presented a 24-page paper at a Royal Geographic Society meeting in 1904, postulating the end of closed political-economic systems that could be insulated from global trends. His paper is still seen as the foundation of the modern science of geopolitics.

All the newest propositions advanced as modern strategic concepts—whether advanced as "planning," "management," or "leadership"—can be found in these earlier geopolitical works and the works of military science.

In addition to geopolitical concepts, the serious student of the strategic concept should consider the implications of what is called "general systems theory" at it mirrors the macro concerns of the strategic concept, addressing the omnipresent features of biological, behavioral, and sociological fields in multivariable interaction (Bertalanffy 1955, 1967). One frequently overlooked, perhaps even now fading cornerstone of management theory, contingency theory (see Ginsberg and Venkatraman 1985), draws directly on general systems theory (Lawrence and Lorsch 1967). The multivariate, contingency interaction has been described as follows:

> The contingency view of organizations and their management suggests that an organization is a system composed of subsystems and delineated by identifiable boundaries from its environmental suprasystem. The contingency view seeks to understand the interrelationships within and among subsystems as well as between the organization and its environment and to define patterns of relationships or configurations of variables. It emphasizes the multivariate nature of organizations and attempts to understand how organizations operate under varying conditions and in specific circumstances. Contingency views are ultimately directed toward suggesting organizational designs and managerial actions most appropriate to specific situations (Kast and Rosenzweig 1974, p. ix).

It is still the challenge of the strategic concept: to respond to environmental and organizational complexity in practical ways that will result in attaining mission (success) with the acquisition of resources (prosperity). Much of this report attempts to take the complexity apart one piece at a time, examine that piece, then put it back together with case examples. A part of the complexity is imbedded in the many conceptual models of planning.

Planning Models
Although neither a proven best model nor a pure model of planning exists, six quasi-models or approaches to planning

have been identified in the literature (Peterson 1980, p. 127). The following outline is a summary of Peterson's six models.

Formal-rational model
The most frequent form of planning is described as one built upon a rational/scientific, step-to-step paradigm (see figure 17).

Organizational development model
The organizational development model may start with the same steps as the formal-rational model, but it is far less concerned

FIGURE 17

FORMAL-RATIONAL MODEL

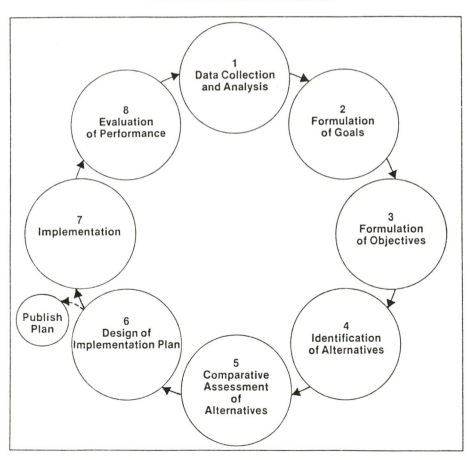

with the formality of the planning process itself and the decisions about goals and is more concerned with understanding the institution as a social or human system. Planning is viewed as a process of learning for all members of the institution. The primary emphasis is internal—focusing on the members themselves.

Technocratic/empirical model
This pseudomodel relies on rational techniques embedded in such systems as management by objective, Delphi surveys, management information systems, and various performance budgeting systems. Implicit in the approaches of such empirical techniques is the fundamental assumption that the basic units of a college or university are quantifiable, measurable resources that can be carefully tracked and directed.

Philosophical synthesis model
Strictly speaking, the philosophical synthesis model is not a model as illustrated in figure 17. As a planning device, this "model" requires asking fundamental questions about the present and future nature of society, humankind, and knowledge. It assesses the mission of the institution. The emphasis is on reasoned discussion, debate, and persuasion. While not well understood, this form of planning is believed to have resulted in such new institutions as Hampshire College, the Evergreen State College, and Empire State College (Peterson 1980).

Political advocacy model
One process of reaching decisions about resource deployment includes issues arising around which interest groups converge and attempt to influence others. Eventually, the interest groups manage to translate the issue into legislation by a recognized planning or governance group, and it is enacted (see Baldridge 1971).

Coordinated anarchy
The underlying assumption of this model is that professionals in autonomous units are best able to foster progress in their domain. The institution adopting this planning process is described as an organized anarchy (Cohen and March 1974).

These forms of planning are present in varying degrees in each institution, which otherwise tends to operate with one model dominating.

Organizational Behavior Models

Organizational behavior here is meant to mean how individuals working together play out their roles. Five primary models are found in colleges and universities (Cope 1985a).

- The *collegial model* (Millett 1978) assumes a collegium of scholars participating fully in decision making. This model presumably works where a shared sense of values, commitment to the institution, a spirit of cooperation, and a view that there is not much if any hierarchy are present. "Let us meet and talk until we can agree" is the dominant mode of interaction.
- The *bureaucratic model* gives more attention to a formal organizational structure, with roles, predetermined regulations, and set procedures. "Let us see what the faculty code book says, then make a proposal through channels."
- The *political model*, in contrast to both the previous ones, assumes that a conflict of goals, values, and preferences is present and natural. Decisions are based upon negotiated compromises arrived at informally and verified through the formal organizational processes (Baldridge 1971). "Let us see if we can get the arts and sciences faculty to join us before we . . . . "
- The *organized anarchy model* (Cohen and March 1974) sees the institution, because of ambiguous goals, systems of rewards, and market connectiveness, unable to manage itself rationally. "Let us agree it is a hopeless situation if we try to get any agreement, so we might as well do whatever each of us wants to do, when we want to do it and how we want to do it."
- The *rational model*, in contrast to the organized anarchy model, sees opportunities for strategic choices that are logically determined by using management information systems, environmental scanning, and similar techniques borrowed from industry (Cope 1978, 1981; cf. Enderud 1980). "Let us determine how to shift resources after the institutional research office and consultants provide us with the information."

Given that the strategic concept as applied by most authorities (but not this author) involves the total institution inside and outside, it may be appropriate to rename the "strategy" concept, as has been done here and there in this report. Calling it the "contextual" concept is preferable (Cope 1985a), as we are dealing with "the organizational context for teaching and learning" (Peterson et al. 1986). Throughout this report, to approach a synthesis of models, "contextual" has been linked with "strategic."

A *contextual model* recognized two contexts: external and internal. The external context refers to the forces operating in the environment beyond the institution. The internal context refers to the values, strengths, weaknesses, and history of the institution: its behavioral norms. The internal (figure 1) consists of the structure, rewards, culture, and controls of the enterprise. Strategic planning in the contextual model weaves the internal context into external anticipated environments.

Others have attempted synthesis. One of the more valuable syntheses of the many competing planning and organizational behavior paradigms is Chaffee's (1984, 1985). She observed three systems of strategy (linear, adaptive, and interpretive), and Chaffee and Tierney (1988) describe them in a familiar

FIGURE 18
THE EVOLUTION OF STRATEGIC DECISION MAKING

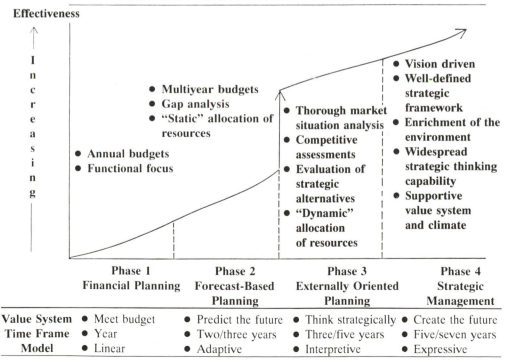

	Phase 1 Financial Planning	Phase 2 Forecast-Based Planning	Phase 3 Externally Oriented Planning	Phase 4 Strategic Management
Value System	● Meet budget	● Predict the future	● Think strategically	● Create the future
Time Frame	● Year	● Two/three years	● Three/five years	● Five/seven years
Model	● Linear	● Adaptive	● Interpretive	● Expressive

context by analogy. Linear systems are like the skeleton in which characteristics are easy to identify and are highly predictable. The location and nature of a break in the skeletal system is easy to identify, and the consequences are predictable. These properties make linear systems to strategy predictable, rational, and goal oriented. But strategy can also be adaptive. Just as people adapt to circumstances and changes, institutions by perceiving of the external environment as a complex, ever-changing set of constituency changes, use an adaptive strategy to realign resources to adapt to the new environment. Institutional structure is changed to meet environmental exigencies. The third system in the analogy recognizes that people are cultural and social. They receive, process, and send messages. They have values. Institutions are thus interpretive systems seeking to understand the institution and its environment. And each approach to strategy contributes to a college or university's effectiveness. (Chaffee and Tierney 1988).

Depending upon one's angle of vision, other variations could be suggested. Organizational saga, for example, does not fit easily any of the above paradigms/models/systems, but it may fit a fourth level in the evolution of strategic decision making (see figure 18). In working with colleges of home economics, Cope (1987) has attempted to define better Glueck's four-phase system (1980) and extend Chaffee's three-level system (1985) into an even more useful fourth level or phase (figure 18).

It is suggested that beyond Chaffee's interpretive level exists an expressive level, one in which the participants in an organization not only interpret their present situation (what is) but seek to strive to fulfill a vision of what can be by creating a vision-driven, strategic framework for competing for resources in future environments. Glueck's strategic management phase is enriched by extending it to an expressive level.

In addition to seeing the strategy concept at four levels, it may be positioned between the two major lines of teaching and research found in schools of management: applied and theoretical management (Cope et al. 1987).

The concept of applied management as it is applied in colleges and universities should largely draw on the central tenet that the best fit is between anticipated environmental conditions and institutional capability. The central variables are the institution's capabilities (strengths and weaknesses) and the trends in the environment (opportunities and threats). The challenge is to find or create a strategic fit to ensure the institution's vitality.

The emphasis is largely applied. [See Andrews (1971), Steiner (1979a, 1979b), and—particularly—Bourgeois (1985) for the origins of the "applied school."]

On the other hand, the "theory school" draws fundamentally on a contingency theory paradigm positing that degrees of turbulence in the environment determine the best institutional structures and best administrative practices for achieving vitality. The central variables are changes in the way environments are perceived, the complexities of environments, the goal orientations and decision styles of institutional participants. The scholar's challenge is to learn how the human organization behaves. The emphasis is largely research. [See Lawrence and Lorsch (1967), Pennings (1975), and again, Bourgeois (1985).]

In conclusion:

Whether identified as "strategic planning," as most of the literature does, or as "contextual planning," as Cope does, the substance of the strategic concept follows a path between these two schools of thought (applied and theory), draws heavily on Thompson's notion (1967) of coalignment, and emphasizes the role of vision (Bennis and Nanus 1985; Haulman 1984) to fuse the many variables competing for attention. The strategic/contextual models thus attempt to blend the applied strategic management and organizational theory perspectives. From the strategic management perspective, the competitive circumstances and the strategic position of the academic enterprise are merged with the human process emphases of organizational theory (Cope et al. 1987, p. 7).

A Summary of Foundations

The strategy concept developed from a long and deep underpinning in the geopolitical sciences and biologically based, open-system disciplines. The biologically based underpinnings point to the importance of finding the niche. The geopolitical sciences offer clues to how to maintain vitality *in the niche* and offer clues to the means of *enlarging the niche*. Cultural anthropology and psychology probably have much to contribute to the strategy concept as well; however, except for Mitroff (1983), little has been suggested from these disciplines.

But ultimately it is probably the arts and humanities that will provide the most valuable insights into the illusive interpretation of the strategic concept. Perhaps this small work will advance the strategic perspective somewhat.

REFERENCES

The Educational Resources Information Center (ERIC) Clearinghouse
on Higher Education abstracts and indexes the current literature on
higher education for inclusion in ERIC's data base and announcement
in ERIC's monthly bibliographic journal, *Resources in Education*
(RIE). Most of these publications are available through the ERIC
Document Reproduction Service (EDRS). For publications cited in this
bibliography that are available from EDRS, ordering number and price
are included. Readers who wish to order a publication should write to
the ERIC Document Reproduction Service, 3900 Wheeler Avenue,
Alexandria, Virginia 22304. (Phone orders with VISA or MasterCard
are taken at 800/227-ERIC or 703/823-0500.) When ordering, please
specify the document (ED) number. Documents are available as noted
in microfiche (MF) and paper copy (PC). Because prices are subject to
change, it is advisable to check the latest issue of *Resources in
Education* for current cost based on the number of pages in the
publication.

References are partially annotated to direct attention to literature that
may serve particular interests, to call attention to trenchant works, and
to comment on the development of thinking among authors who are
consistently adding new dimensions to the concept of strategic
planning.

Abell, Derek. 1980. *Defining the Business: The Starting Point of
Strategic Planning*. Englewood Cliffs, N.J.: Prentice-Hall.
Seminal observations about defining the essence of what an
enterprise is all about and how it relates to its client base.

Ackoff, Russell L. 1970. *A Concept of Corporate Planning*. New
York: John Wiley & Sons.
Perhaps the best analysis of the fundamental assumptions of the
planning function. Building on Ansoff (below), the book also
contains insights into operations analysis from the standpoint of
corporations.

Ahumada, Martin M., and Hefferlin, J.B. Lon. 1986. "Sources of
Assistance." *Environmental Scanning for Strategic Leadership*,
edited by P. Callan. New Directions for Institutional Research No.
52. San Francisco: Jossey-Bass.

Andrews, K.R. 1971. *The Concept of Corporate Strategy*.
Homewood, Ill.: Dow Jones–Irwin.

Ansoff, Igor H. 1965. *Corporate Strategy: An Analytical Approach to
Business Policy for Growth and Expansion*. New York: McGraw-
Hill.
Ansoff has been one of the leading analysts of the essence of the
strategic concept from its earliest days in the mid-1960s. Much of
his thinking and most other leading authors have been influenced by
this 1965 book. Making the primary point that strategic choices are
those dealing with the environment, he relates strategic,

administrative, and operating decisions as three classes of decisions. Ansoff also signaled the move from strategic *planning* to strategic *management* in 1976 in a book coauthored with Declerick and Hayes (see below).

———. 1969. *Business Strategy*. Baltimore: Penguin Books.

———. 1979. *Strategic Management*. New York: Halstead Press.

———. 1984. *Implementing Strategic Management*. Englewood Cliffs, N.J.: Prentice-Hall.

Ansoff, Igor H.; Declerick, Roger; and Hayes, Robert. 1976. *From Strategic Planning to Strategic Management*. New York: John Wiley & Sons.

Just as Ansoff's *Corporate Strategy* was a forerunner in integrating the concept of strategic *planning*, this book reintegrates the field, incorporating *management* as the integrating concept. See also Ansoff's *Strategic Management* (above).

Anthony, R. 1965. *Planning and Control Systems*. Cambridge, Mass.: Harvard Graduate School of Business.

A seminal work defining the purposes of information systems.

Arns, R.G., and Curran, F.A. 1982. "Information System Requirements for Strategic Planning and Implementation." Paper presented at the 1982 CAUSE National Conference, Hilton Head Island, South Carolina, December.

Astley, W. Graham, and Fombrun, Charles. 1983. "Collective Strategy: Social Ecology of Organizational Environments." *Academy of Management Review* 8(4): 576–87.

A scholar's article dealing with relationships among organizations in an ecology of organizations, particularly the constraining effect of environments on an enterprise's choices. For the serious student of strategy.

Baker, Michael E. 1982. "A Distributed Information Strategy." Paper presented at an Association for Institutional Research forum, 14 May, Denver, Colorado. ED 220033. 26 pp. MF–$1.07; PC–$5.79.

A descriptive paper about how a department-based management information system serves the strategic planning functions of Carnegie-Mellon University.

Baldridge, J.V. 1971. *Power and Conflict in the University*. New York: John Wiley & Sons.

The result of a dissertation and a major contribution to understanding the political nature of organizational behavior. Widely referenced.

Below, Patrick; Morrisey, George; and Acomb, Betty. 1988. *The Executive Guide to Strategic Planning*. San Francisco: Jossey-Bass.

An excellent, practical, and easy-to-read introduction to strategic planning from the perspective of the CEO.

Bennis, Warren, and Nanus, Burt. 1985. *Leaders: The Strategies for*

Taking Charge. New York: Harper & Row.

Includes many of the same points made in this report, except that the perspective is more that of the organizational leader. Touts top-down leadership. See also the authors' observations about how organizations learn in "Organizational Learning: The Management of the Collective Self." *New Management* 3 (1985): 6–13.

Bertalanffy, Ludwig von. 1955. "General Systems Theory." *Main Currents in Modern Thought* 11: 75–83.

———. 1967. *Robots, Men, and Minds: Psychology in the Modern World*. New York: George Braziller.

Birnbaum, Robert. 1983. *Maintaining Diversity in Higher Education*. San Francisco: Jossey-Bass.

Bolman, L.G., and Deal, T.E. 1985. *Modern Approaches to Understanding and Managing Organizations*. San Francisco: Jossey-Bass.

Recognizing that organizational theory is complex yet attempting to create useful models for seeing the reality of how people in organizations behave, the authors offer four conceptual frames, with illustrations, to sort out behavior in organizations: structural, human resources, political, and symbolic.

Borton, Nancy. 1987a. "Background and Rationale for a University-Affiliated High-Technology Incubator in Seattle." A mimeographed administrative briefing paper. Seattle: University of Washington.

———. 1987b. "Case Analysis of the Formulation of Ideas, Implementation, and Economic Impact of Four Community College Initiatives in Washington State: A Pilot Project." Mimeographed. Seattle: University of Washington.

Bourgeois, L.J., III. 1984. "Strategic Implementation: Five Approaches to an Elusive Phenomenon." *Strategic Management Journal* 5: 241–64.

Five approaches to implement organizational strategy.

———. 1985. "Strategic Goals, Perceived Uncertainty, and Economic Performance in Volatile Environments." *Academy of Management Journal* 28(3): 548–73.

Burns, James M. 1978. *Leadership*. New York: Harper & Row.

A trenchant analysis of the requirements of leadership in complex organizations in a complex society.

Callan, Patrick M., ed. 1986. *Environmental Leadership for Strategic Leadership*. New Directions for Institutional Research No. 52. San Francisco: Jossey-Bass.

Cameron, Kim S. 1978. "Measuring Organizational Effectiveness in Institutions of Higher Education." *Administrative Science Quarterly* 23: 604–29.

Cameron and his usual coauthors (Chaffee, Peterson, and Whetten) are among the most able at translating general theories of organizations from business firms to higher education.

————. 1981. "The Enigma of Organizational Effectiveness." New Directions for Program Evaluation No. 11. San Francisco: Jossey-Bass.

A conceptual piece contrasting four models of organizational effectiveness.

————. 1983. "Strategic Responses to Conditions of Decline: Higher Education and the Private Sector." *Journal of Higher Education* 54(4): 359–80.

————. 1984a. "Organizational Adaptation and Higher Education." *Journal of Higher Education* 55: 122–44.

————. 1984b. "The Paradox in Institutional Renewal." In *Leadership and Institutional Renewal*, edited by Ralph Davis. San Francisco: Jossey-Bass.

Cameron, Kim S., and Chaffee, Ellen E. 1983. *The Aftermath of Decline*. Washington, D.C.: National Institute of Education. ED 271087. 41 pp. MF–$1.07; PC–$5.79.

A study of probable decline in enrollments and revenues among a sample of 334 colleges over five years (1977 to 1981).

————. , eds. 1985. "A Special Issue on Institutional Effectiveness." *Review of Higher Education* 9.

Cameron, Kim S., and Whetten, David A. 1981. "Perception of Organizational Effectiveness over Organizational Life Cycles." *Administrative Science Quarterly* 6(4): 525–44.

A report on a study of how students perceived organizational effectiveness as the organizations developed.

Caples, Virginia, ed. 1987. *Confronting Today's Challenges: Positioning for Future Challenges*. Proceedings of a joint conference of the Association of Administrators of Home Economics and the National Council of Administrators of Home Economics, 18–21 February, San Francisco, California. Available from the author, Division of Home Economics, Alabama A&M University, Normal, Alabama 35762.

Carroll, James, et al. 1984. "Revising a College's Planning System: Translating Theory into Practice." *Planning for Higher Education* 13(1): 23–28.

A case study of the planning, budgeting, and monitoring system at the National Technical Institute for the Deaf at the Rochester Institute of Technology. Suggests that the system is forward looking, anticipating potential crises.

Chaffee, Ellen E. 1984. "Successful Strategic Management in Small Private Colleges." *Journal of Higher Education* 55(2): 212–38.

An examination of two sets of colleges that experienced severe financial difficulties in the 1970s. One set made dramatic recoveries; the other set did not. The more resilient group pursued adaptive and interpretive strategies; the less resilient group followed linear strategies.

————. 1985. "The Concept of Business Strategy: From Business to Higher Education." In *Higher Education: Handbook of Theory and Research*, Vol. 1, edited by John Smart. Washington, D.C.: American Educational Research Association.

Chaffee has developed one of the more useful paradigms for examining the strategic concept, seeing strategy conforming to linear, adaptive, and interpretive models. An article illustrating how the concepts have moved from the business community to the academy.

Chaffee, Ellen E., and Tierney, William G. 1988. *Collegiate Cultures and Leadership Strategies*. New York: Macmillan.

Seven in-depth case studies about the realities of colleges and universities as socially constructed organizations acted upon by leaders who may apply a variety of leadership strategies.

Chandler, Alfred. 1962. *Strategy and Structure: Chapters in the History of the American Industrial Enterprise*. Cambridge, Mass.: MIT Press.

Cleveland, Harlan. 1985a. *The Knowledge Executive*. New York: Truman Talley Books/E.P. Dutton.

Advanced thinking about the private and public requirements of the information age and a philosophical stance that is clearly democratic. As nations are becoming even more knowledge based, this book addresses the changing roles of leadership and participation in modern organizations.

————. January/February 1985b. "Twilight of Hierarchy: Speculations on the Global Information Society." *Public Administration Review*.

Cleveland's writing in recent years has concentrated on what information will mean to organizations, leadership, and societal change. His important book is *The Knowledge Executive* (see above).

Clugston, Richard M., Jr. 1986. "Strategic Planning in an Organized Anarchy: The Emperor's New Clothes?" Paper presented at the Annual Meeting of the Association for the Study of Higher Education, 20–23 February, San Antonio, Texas. ED 268 902. 35 pp. MF–$1.07; PC–$5.79.

A study of how strategic planning affected the allocation of resources among 42 departments at the University of Minnesota, which found that strategic planning did influence how resources moved from low- to high-priority programs.

————. 1987. "Strategic Adaptation in an Organized Anarchy: Priority Setting and Resource Allocation in the Liberal Arts College of a Public Research University." Doctoral dissertation, University of Minnesota.

Cohen, Michael O., and March, James. 1974. *Leadership and Ambiguity: The American College President*. New York: McGraw-Hill.

Cope, Robert G. 1978. *Strategic Policy Planning: A Guide for College and University Administrators*. Englewood, Colo.: Ireland Corp.

The first general attempt in higher education to adapt the business community's strategic planning techniques to colleges and universities. Since this first publication, Cope's approach has become decidedly less linear.

————. 1981. *Strategic Planning, Management, and Decision Making*. Washington, D.C.: American Association for Higher Education. ED 217 825. 75 pp. MF–$1.07; PC–$7.73.

A monograph tracing the history of strategic planning and suggesting a conceptual framework for its present-day elements.

————. 1985a. "A Contextual Model to Encompass the Strategic Planning Concept: Introducing a Newer Paradigm." *Planning in Higher Education* 13(3): 13–20.

An article urging an adoption of a term other than "strategy" for the use of colleges and universities. "Context" is suggested, and a particular model for contextual planning is recommended.

————. January 1985b. "Six Management Propositions for Economic Vitality in the Pacific Basin." *Asia-Pacific Journal of Management* 81–95.

A summary of the contributions of geographers and naval historians to strategic management, applying their propositions to state and national economic development in the emerging Pacific region.

————. 1986. "Information System Requirements for Strategic Choices." In *Environmental Scanning for Strategic Leadership*, edited by P.M. Callan. New Directions for Institutional Research No. 52. San Francisco: Jossey-Bass.

Recommendation of a strategic triangle concept for gathering information used to make strategic choices and for control functions.

————. 1987. "Planning for the Future, Strategically: The Case of the Bourbon College of Home Economics." In *Confronting Today's Challenges: Positioning for Future Challenges*, edited by Virginia Caples. Proceedings of a joint conference of the Association of Administrators of Home Economics and the National Council of Administrators of Home Economics, 18–21 February, San Francisco, California.

Most of the proceedings focus on how the strategic concept applies to colleges of home economics. Several case examples are included: the hypothetical Bourbon College and the real home economics programs at the University of Missouri and Oregon State University. The many selections contain many fine examples of environmental scanning for trends affecting people from birth to death.

————. 1988. *Enterprise and Environment*. Oxford, Ohio: Planning Forum.

Recognizing the growth of professional staff in organizations, this book illustrates how they can participate in the formulation of the strategies of their enterprise. Most of the book's focus is not on colleges and universities.

Cope, Robert; Meredith, Mark; Lenning, Oscar; and Borton, Nancy. 1987. "Strategic Planning, Management, and Leadership: Clarification and Case Examples." Paper presented at a conference of the Pacific Northwest Association for Institutional Research, 12–13 November, Eugene, Oregon.

Cyert, Richard M. 1981. "Management Science and University Management." New Directions for Higher Education No. 9. San Francisco: Jossey-Bass.

Davis, Peter. 31 October 1984. "Seminars with Pictures." *Wall Street Journal*.

Drake, Rodman L. 1986. "Innovative Structures for Managing Change." *Planning Review* 14(6): 18–22.

The model illustrated in this report (used in the author's New York consulting firm) is especially useful for seeing the whole process of strategic planning and management.

Drucker, Peter F. 1974. *Management: Tasks, Responsibilities, and Practices*. New York: Harper & Row.

———. 1985. *Innovative and Entrepreneurship*. London: William Heinemann.

Drucker extols the entrepreneurial society, provides a road map to the discovery of opportunity, and suggests basic strategies for firms or product lines based on practical wisdom: be first with the most, hit where they are not, build on an ecological niche, innovate.

Enarson, Harold L. 1975. "The Art of Planning." *Educational Record* 56: 170–74.

Enderud, Harold. 1980. "Administrative Leadership in Organized Anarchies." *International Journal of Institutional Management in Higher Education* 4: 235–53.

Filerman, Gary L. 1984. "Socioeconomic Trends and Strategic Planning for Health Services Education." *Educational Record* 65(4): 4–8.

Frances, Carol; Huxel, George; Meyerson, Joel; and Park, Dabney. 1987. *Strategic Decision Making: Key Questions and Indicators for Trustees*. Washington, D.C.: Association of Governing Boards of Universities and Colleges. HE 021 337. 82 pp. MF–$1.07; PC–$10.13.

Written for the college trustee, this easy-to-read manual unfortunately simply uses the word "strategy" as a cover for addressing a wide variety of nevertheless important management decision areas.

Freed, Jann E. 1987. "Relationships among Indicators of Institutional

Viability and Variables Associated with Planning Processes in Small, Independent, Liberal Arts Institutions." Doctoral dissertation, Iowa State University.

Gill, Judith I. 1987. "Higher Education and State Government in Michigan: A Historical and Organizational Analysis of the Relationship from 1950 to 1971." Doctoral dissertation, University of Michigan.

Ginsberg, Ari, and Venkatraman, N. 1985. "Contingency Perspectives of Organizational Strategy: A Critical Review of the Empirical Research." *Academy of Management Review* 10(3): 421–34.

Those thinking of doing research on the strategy concept will find in this article advice on both theoretical and methodological issues.

Glueck, Frederick. 1980. *Management and Business Policy*. New York: McGraw-Hill.

Gray, Daniel H. January/February 1986. "Uses and Misuses of Strategic Planning." *Harvard Business Review*: 89–97.

This article may be seen as the response to two critical reviews of strategic planning by *Fortune* and *Business Week*. Gray's main point is that "there is nothing wrong with strategic planning if you do it right." Most of his observations are consistent with the points made in this report.

Green, Kinsey B. 1987. "The Future of Home Economics in Higher Education." In *Confronting Today's Challenges: Positioning for Future Challenges*, edited by Virginia Caples. Proceedings of a joint conference of the Association of Administrators of Home Economics and the National Council of Administrators of Home Economics, 18–21 February, San Francisco, California.

Groff, Warren H. 1986. "Institutional Research and Assessment of the External Environment." In *Applying Institutional Research in Decision Making*, edited by J. Losak. New Directions for Community Colleges No. 56. San Francisco: Jossey-Bass.

Guskin, Alan E., and Bassis, Michael A. 1986. "Leadership Style and Institutional Renewal." New Directions for Higher Education No. 13. San Francisco: Jossey-Bass.

Hackman, Judith Dozier. 1985. "Power and Centrality in the Allocation of Resources in Colleges and Universities." *Administrative Science Quarterly* 30: 61–77.

Halstead, Kent, ed. 1987. *Higher Education Bibliographic Handbook*. Washington, D.C.: Research Associates.

———. 1988. *Higher Education Bibliographic Handbook*. Washington, D.C.: Research Associates.

An annual guide to the best literature in higher education.

Hart, Stuart; Boroush, Mark; Enk, Gordon; and Hornick, William. 1985. "Managing Complexity through Consensus Mapping: Technology for Structuring of Group Decisions." *Academy of*

Management Review 10(3): 587–600.

Expands on the strawman model of group decision making.

Haulman, B. 1984. "A Test of Cope's Contextual Model." Technical Paper. Seattle: University of Washington, School of Education.

Postulates an empirical test of Cope's contextual planning model (see Cope 1985a above).

Hayes, Robert H. November/December 1985. "Strategic Planning: Forward in Reverse." *Harvard Business Review*: 111–19.

A thoughtful article about the traditional ends-ways-means model of strategic planning, which, Hayes argues, is logical but wrong in turbulent environments. He recommends instead the adoption of a model that builds on capacity (means) and points the enterprise toward ends, as a compass points direction of travel.

―――. 1986. "Strategic Planning for Information Resources in the Research University." *Research Quarterly* 25(4): 427–31.

A description of the way the strategy concept was used to address the long-term development of the library and information resources at UCLA.

Hearn, James C., and Heydinger, Richard. "Scanning the University's External Environment—Objectives, Constraints, Possibilities." *Journal of Higher Education* 56(4): 419–45.

Heydinger, Richard B. 1983. "Using Program Priorities to Make Retrenchment Decisions: The Case of the University of Minnesota." Paper prepared for the Southern Regional Education Board, Atlanta, Georgia. ED 230 119. 9 pp. MF–$1.07; PC–$3.85.

Illustrates how six criteria (quality, connectedness, integration, uniqueness, demand, and cost effectiveness) were used to adjust allocations among departments at the University of Minnesota in response to financial cutbacks in the early 1980s.

―――. , ed. 1980. "Academic Planning for the 80s." New Directions for Institutional Research No. 7. San Francisco: Jossey-Bass.

Hoadley, J.A., and Zimmer, B.E. 1982. "A Corporate Planning Approach to Institutional Management: A Preliminary Report on the RMIT Experience." *Journal of Tertiary Education Administration* 4(1): 15–26.

Jacob, Julie. 1987. "Community College Leadership: Creating Partnerships with Business and Industry." Mimeographed. Seattle: University of Washington.

Jedamus, Paul; Peterson, Marvin; and Associates. 1980. *Improving Academic Management: A Handbook of Planning and Institutional Research*. San Francisco: Jossey-Bass.

Contains the most thoughtful analysis of the concept of planning among institutions of higher education in the educational literature in a chapter entitled "Analyzing Alternative Approaches to

Planning," which describes the conceptual bases of planning and six models for planning and integrates strategies and leadership styles.

Johnson, Lynn G. 1984. *The High-Technology Connection: Academic/ Industrial Cooperation for Economic Growth*. ASHE-ERIC Higher Education Report No. 6. Washington, D.C.: Association for the Study of Higher Education. ED 255 130. 129 pp. MF–$1.07; PC– $14.01.

Perhaps the best summary of what is happening among institutions of higher education and the business community as they work together to contribute to economic development. Includes concepts and case examples.

Jonsen, Richard W. 1984. "Small Colleges Cope with the Eighties." *Journal of Higher Education* 55(2): 171–83.

———. 1986. "The Environmental Context for Postsecondary Education." In *Environmental Scanning for Strategic Leadership*, edited by P. Callan. New Directions for Institutional Research No. 54. San Francisco: Jossey-Bass.

Kanter, Rosabeth Moss. 1981. "Power, Leadership, and Participatory Management." *Theory into Practice* 20(4): 219–24.

Women authors make an apparently larger contribution to the literature of analyses of power. See, for example, Hackman (above).

Kast, F.E., and Rosenzweig, J.E. 1974. *Organization and Management*. Englewood Cliffs, N.J.: Prentice-Hall.

A systems view of organizations, including a substantial section on higher education.

Kauffman, Joseph. 1984. "Profile of the Presidency in the Next Decade." *Educational Record* 65(2): 6–8.

Keller, George. 1983. *Academic Strategy: The Management Revolution in American Higher Education*. Baltimore: Johns Hopkins University Press.

Probably the largest-selling book ever written about planning and management in higher education. Based on sound concepts. Contains good case examples but not particularly useful on how to go about the planning process.

Keller, Robert. 1985. "Commitment to Focus: The University of Minnesota's Plan for Excellence." Mimeographed. Minneapolis: University of Minnesota.

Kerr, Clark. 1982. "Crises in Leadership." *AGB Reports* 24(4): 4–7.

Kolenbrander, Harold M. 1983. "Internal Politics and Strategies of Implementing Change with Limited Resources." *Planning for Higher Education* 11(4): 5–9.

A wise, honest, and principled approach to working with the faculty to achieve greater productivity and curricular change by an experienced, patient administrator. Wisdom similar to Mintzberg 1987 (below) applied directly to higher education.

Kotler, Philip. 1982. *Marketing for Nonprofit Organizations.* Englewood Cliffs, N.J.: Prentice-Hall.

Regarded as the best guide to thinking strategically from a marketing perspective available to the not-for-profit sector.

Kotler, Phillip, and Fox, Karen F.A. 1985. *Strategic Planning for Educational Organizations.* Englewood Cliffs, N.J.: Prentice-Hall.

Kotler, Philip, and Murphy, P.E. 1981. "Strategic Planning for Higher Education." *Journal of Higher Education* 52(5): 470–89.

A widely quoted article that nevertheless may represent a set of ideas that are too close to the profit-making firm for use in strategic planning or management in colleges and universities. From a conceptual standpoint, Kotler 1982 (above) is more useful.

Lawrence, P., and Lorsch, J. 1967. *Organization and Environment.* Boston: Harvard Business School, Division of Research.

Leinberger, Christopher, and Lockwood, Charles. October 1986. "How Business Is Reshaping America." *Atlantic Monthly*: 43–52.

A particularly insightful article about the dynamics of urban development. Must reading for anyone doing large-scale public or private planning in an urban environment.

Leister, Douglas V. July/August 1975. "Identifying Institutional Clientele: Applied Metamarketing in Higher Education Administration." *Journal of Higher Education* 46: 381–98.

Lelong, Donald, and Shirley, Robert. 1984. "Planning: Identifying the Focal Points for Action." *Planning for Higher Education* 12(4).

Lenning, Oscar T. 1987. "Successful Strategic Planning." Presentation at the Annual Conference of the Christian College Coalition Academic Deans, February, Chicago, Illinois.

Lenz, R.T., and Lyles, Marjorie. 1986. "Managing Human Problems in Strategic Planning Systems." *Journal of Business Strategy* 6(4): 57–66.

Identification of the most common human problems confronting a planning/change process and suggestions of ways to minimize the effects of those problems.

Lindbloom, C.E. Spring 1959. "The Science of Muddling Through." *Public Administration Review* 19:79–88.

Luthans, Fred. 1986. "Fifty Years Later: What Do We Really Know about Managers and Managing?" Presidential Address at the Annual Meeting of the Academy of Management, 15 August, Chicago, Illinois.

A summary of findings from a four-year study of 300 managers. The study, whose dependent variables were success and effectiveness, found that networking was related to success, communication and human resource skills were related to effectiveness, and traditional management skills were related to neither.

McCune, Shirley. 1986. *Guide to Strategic Planning for Educators*. Alexandria, Va.: Association for Supervision and Curriculum.

Apparently the first monograph on how to plan strategically for grades K–12. Conceptually sound and easy to follow.

Mackinder, Halford. 1904. "The Geographic Pivot of History." Paper presented before the Royal Geographic Society. Reprinted in *Democratic Ideals and Reality* (1951) and in *The Scope and Methods of Geography* (1919). London: Royal Geographic Society.

Mahan, Alfred. 1890. *The Influence of Sea Power on History, 1660–1783*. Boston: Little, Brown, and New York: Hill & Wang (1967).

Meredith, Mark. 1984. "A Jump Ahead...in Which Direction?" *New Directions for Institutional Research* 11(4): 87–92.

————. 1985. "Strategic Planning and Management: A Survey of Practices and Benefits in Higher Education." Paper presented at the Annual Forum of the Association for Institutional Research, Portland, Oregon. ED 267 697. 63 pp. MF–$1.07; PC–$7.73.

Meredith, Mark; Cope, Robert; and Lenning, Oscar. 1987. "Differentiating Bona Fide Strategic Planning from Other Planning." Technical Paper. Boulder, Colo.: University of Colorado. ED 287 329. 26 pp. MF–$1.07; PC–$5.79.

A report on phase two of a three-phase study to discover what proportion of a sample of approximately 100 institutions are actually planning to use strategic concepts.

Meredith, Mark; Lenning, Oscar; and Cope, Robert. 1988. "After Six Years, Does Strategic Planning Make Any Difference?" Paper presented at a forum of the Association for Institutional Research, May, Phoenix, Arizona.

After six years, institutions planning strategically were compared with those not following bona fide strategic planning. Institutions planning strategically reported greater satisfaction and more rapid gains in money resources. Institutions not planning strategically were actually poorer when costs were apportioned per faculty member and per student and corrected by the Higher Education Price Index.

Miller, James L. 1983. "Strategic Planning as Pragmatic Adaptation." *Planning for Higher Education* 12(1): 17–24.

Millett, John. 1978. *New Structures of Campus Power*. San Francisco: Jossey-Bass.

Mintzberg, Henry. July/August 1987. "Crafting Strategy." *Harvard Business Review*: 66–77.

One of the two best articles in *HBR* for 1987. Sage advice on the reality of how strategy develops in organizations.

Mitroff, Ian. 1983. *Stakeholders of the Organizational Mind*. San

Francisco: Jossey-Bass.

Another description of the multiplicity and complexity of interests, institutions, actors, and stake holders bearing on organizational management. What is less usual is Mitroff's metaphysical notion of stake holders themselves. Where do they come from? How are they organized? How do they influence? As usual, Mitroff is highly critical of conventional social science with its perpetual concern for empirical trivialities and its narrow research perspectives.

Morrison, James L. 1987. "Establishing an Environmental Scanning/ Forecasting System to Augment College and University Planning." *Planning for Higher Education* 15(1): 7–22.

Probably the best single source to understand Morrison's careful approach to examining the environment. Particularly useful for helping to organize information. Valuable examples from colleges and other organizations.

Morrison, James L., and Cope, Robert G. 1985. "Using Future Research Techniques in Strategic Planning: A Simulation." *Planning for Higher Education* 13(2): 5–9.

Morrison, James L.; Renfro, William L.; and Boucher, Wayne I. 1984. *Futures Research and the Strategic Planning Process: Implications for Higher Education*. ASHE-ERIC Higher Education Report No. 9. Washington, D.C.: Association for the Study of Higher Education. ED 259 692. 141 pp. MF–$1.07; PC–$14.01.

An impressive collection of literature and techniques for doing trends analyses, drawing implications from a variety of futuring techniques.

Naisbitt, John. 1982. *Megatrends: Ten Directions Transforming Our Lives*. New York: Warner Books.

The best-selling book on 10 future patterns in the society, taking the United States into the next century.

Norris, Donald M.; and Poulton, Nick L. 1987. *A Guide for New Planners*. Ann Arbor, Mich.: University of Michigan, Society for College and University Planning.

A guide to what to do and what not to do and a comprehensive bibliography for those new to planning. Not a how-to guide so much as, according to the authors, a road map of the field.

Ohmae, Kenichi. 1982. *The Mind of the Strategist: The Art of Japanese Business*. New York: McGraw-Hill.

A clearly written book by a popular U.S. author and runaway best-selling author in Japan that integrates the fundamental concepts of strategy (positioning, competitor assessment, and so on) into how to think, how to be creative, how to trust intuition. A particularly valuable portion of this book is its attention to illustrations to express key points. Examples range from global firms to local fast-food shops.

———. Winter 1983. "The Strategic Triangle and Business Unit Strategy." *The Mckinsey Quarterly*: 9–24.

Pailthorp, Keith. 1986. "Examples of Strategic Planning at Several Levels." *Environmental Scanning for Strategic Leadership*, edited by P. Callan. New Directions for Institutional Research No. 52. San Francisco: Jossey-Bass.

Parker, Walter. 1986. "Justice, Social Studies, and the Subjectivity/Structure Problem." *Theory and Research in Social Education* 14(4): 277–93.

An exploration of the complex cognitive functions of persons who reason about complex social issues that contains a bibliography identifying major concepts from dialectical reasoning.

Pennings, J.M. 1975. "The Relevance of the Structural-Contingency Model for Organizational Effectiveness." *Administrative Science Quarterly* 20: 393–410.

Peters, T., and Waterman, R. 1982. *In Search of Excellence: Lessons from America's Best-Run Companies*. New York: Harper & Row.

The multimillion-copy best seller on management practices among leading firms. Advances the 7-S formula for an enterprise's success.

Peterson, Marvin W. 1980. "Analyzing Alternative Approaches to Planning." In *Improving Academic Management: A Handbook of Planning and Institutional Research*, edited by Paul Jedamus, Marvin Peterson, and Associates. San Francisco: Jossey-Bass.

Among the most insightful interpretations of how organizational theory applies to planning generally, including a special section on the strategic concept.

———. 1984. "In a Decade of Decline: The Seven Rs of Planning." *Change* 16(4): 42–46.

———. 1986. "Continuity, Challenge, and Change: An Organizational Perspective on Planning Past and Future." *Planning for Higher Education* 14(3): 6–15.

Peterson, Marvin W.; Cameron, Kim S.; Mets, Lisa A.; Jones, Philip; and Ettington, Deborah. 1986. *The Organizational Context for Teaching and Learning: A Review of the Research Literature*. Ann Arbor: University of Michigan, National Center for Research to Improve Postsecondary Teaching and Learning. ED 287 437. 120 pp. MF–$1.07; PC–$12.07.

Probably the most informative set of observations on the pertinent concepts for managing higher education since Jedamus and Peterson 1980 (above). Insightful views on leadership, organizational dynamics, and strategy that go well beyond a simple review of the research literature. The document concludes with a framework for joining strategy and culture that attempts to overcome what the authors (mostly Peterson) view as a literature on the organizational context that is "sparse, confusing, and in a state of conceptual chaos."

Peterson, Marvin, and Mets, Lisa, eds. 1987. *Key Resources on Governance, Management, and Leadership*. San Francisco:

Jossey-Bass.

An excellent guide to references resources for practicing administrators, faculty, and students. A comprehensive work, cutting across nearly all matters of management, planning, and leadership in its 20 chapters.

Pfeffer, J., and Moore, W. 1980. "Power in University Budgeting: A Replication and Extension." *Administration Science Quarterly* 25(4): 637–53.

Pfeffer, J., and Salanick, G. 1974. "Organizational Decision Making as a Political Process: The Case of a University Budget." *Administrative Science Quarterly* 19(1): 135–51.

———. 1978. *The External Control of Organizations: A Resource Dependence Perspective*. New York: Harper & Row.

Porteous, J.D. 1982 "Approaches to Environmental Aesthetics." *Journal of Environmental Psychology* 2: 53–66.

Makes the point that the most powerful sense is vision.

Richardson, Richard C., and Gardner, Don E. 1985. "Designing a Cost-Effective Planning Process." *Planning for Higher Education* 13(2): 10–13.

Rockart, J.F. 1982. "The Changing Role of the Information Systems Executive." *Sloan Management Review* 24(1): 3–13.

Rolf, Bertil. 1987. "The Tacit Dimension of Professional Knowledge: From Higher Education to Profession." *Studies of Higher Education and Research*, a newsletter of the Swedish Research on Higher Education Program, Stockholm.

Romeromorett, Martin, and Riveravargas, Marisa. Spring 1987. "Strategic Planning: A Study Case for the University of Guadalajara." Technical Paper, Seattle: University of Washington, College of Education.

Sapp, Mary M. 1985. "Decision Support Systems for Strategic Planning." *CAUSE/EFFECT* 8(5): 34–39.

A description of how data and graphs were used in the planning process for the University of Miami's five-year strategic plan using microcomputer-based decision support systems.

Schmidtlein, Frank A. 1974. "Decision Process Paradigms in Higher Education." *Educational Researcher* 3: 4–11.

———. 1985. "Institutional Planning: Perspectives and Practices." Grant proposal to the Office of Educational Research and Improvement from the National Center for Postsecondary Governance and Finance, University of Maryland.

Schwartz, Howard. 1987. "Strategic Urban Planning." Paper presented at the 29th Annual Conference of the Association of Collegiate Schools of Planning, 6 November, Los Angeles, California.

Scott, William G., and Hart, David K. 1979. *Organizational America*.

Boston: Houghton Mifflin.

A critical assessment of the condition of American society, where individuals are absorbed into the workings of large and ever larger organizations. Individuals are seen being reshaped for maximizing organizational utility.

Shirley, Robert C. 1983. "Identifying the Levels of Strategy for a College or University." *Long-Range Planning* 16(3): 92–98.

Simon, Herbert. 1987. "Making Management Decisions: The Role of Intuition and Emotion." *Executive* 1(1): 57–64.

Smith, Bea. 1987. "Challenges to New Administrators." In *Confronting Today's Challenges: Positioning for Future Challenges*, edited by Virginia Caples. Proceedings of a joint conference of the Association of Administrators of Home Economics and the National Council of Administrators of Home Economics, 18–21 February, San Francisco, California.

South, S. Spring 1981. "Competitive Advantage: The Cornerstone of Strategic Thinking." *Journal of Business Strategy*.

Ideas and some research findings contributed by 33 educators as to how colleges can cooperate and compete, given the changes through the remainder of the century. Illustrates and applauds the pluralism of American higher education.

Stauffer, Thomas M., ed. 1981. *Competition and Cooperation in American Higher Education*. Washington, D.C.: American Council on Education.

Steeples, D.A. 1986. *Institutional Revival: Case Histories*. New Directions for Higher Education No. 54. San Francisco: Jossey-Bass.

Presidents tell how their institutions (Eckerd College, the University of the Redlands, Birmingham-Southern College, the College of Idaho, Queens College, the New Port College, and Northland College) were redirected to survive. Most of the accounts are from a strategic perspective in which strengths were connected with opportunity. Accounts are presented without theory and demonstrate the importance of risk taking and imagination for successful turnarounds.

Steiner, George A. 1979a. "Contingency Theories of Strategy and Strategic Management." In *Strategic Management: A New View of Business Policy and Planning*, edited by D. Schendel and C.W. Hofer. Boston: Little Brown.

———. 1979b. *Strategic Planning: What Every Manager Must Know*. New York: Free Press.

A popular, succinct, easy-to-read, state-of-the-art book. While it is not technical, it does not give the attention to the environment or group processes that seems necessary.

Stogdill, Ralph. 1974. *Handbook of Leadership*. Glencoe, Ill.: Free Press.

Sullivan, C.H. 1985. "Systems Planning in the Information Age." *Sloan Management Review* 26(2): 3–12.

Sun Zi (Tzu). 1980 trans. *The Art of War*, edited by James Clavall. New York: Delacorte.

Perhaps the first writing about the strategic concept, done by the Chinese general Sun Tzu about 2,500 years ago.

Thompson, J.D. 1967. *Organizations in Action*. New York: McGraw-Hill.

Toffler, Alvin. 1981. *The Third Wave*. New York: William Morrow/Bantam Books.

Toffler's *Future Shock* was a provocative glimpse into our rapidly changing times. This book provides another look into the future as present, mapping civilization's fragile interdependencies.

Toftoy, Charles. 1987. *How CEOs Set Strategic Direction for Their Organizations*. Oxford, Ohio: Planning Forum.

Toll, John S. 1985. "Strategic Planning: An Increasing Priority for Colleges and Universities." *Change* 14(3): 36–37.

A university president claims strategic planning is necessary to assist change.

Trachtenberg, Stephen J. 1985. "Positioning for Survival." *Planning for Higher Education* 13(4): 1–3.

A university president speaks to admissions officers from the strategic perspective. One of the first presidents among college personnel to recognize the value of strategic planning for institutions of higher education.

Uhl, Norman P. 1983. *Using Research for Strategic Planning*. New Directions for Institutional Research No. 37. San Francisco: Jossey-Bass.

Waddell, William. 1976. *The Outline of Strategy*. Oxford, Ohio: Planning Forum.

A highly readable, insightful, and practical guide to many strategic concepts. Particularly useful for identifying general strategic options: segmentation, niche, retrenchment, turnaround, and so on, with many examples from private firms.

Walters, Susan, and Choate, Pat. 1984. *Thinking Strategically: A Primer for Public Leaders*. Washington, D.C.: Council of State Planning Agencies.

An introduction to the concept of strategic planning for those in public agencies whose key point is that strategy must be tailor-made situation by situation, just as it is in business, except that in the public sector politics rather than competition is a major consideration. The key political variables are the perpetual campaign, transient leadership, special interest groups, separation of powers, and the role of the media. Competition enters political parties and among intergovernmental agencies. An issue matrix is useful for ranking decision requirements according to the need for action and the ability of the agency to influence the outcome of the issue.

Weick, Karl E. 1976. "Educational Organizations as Loosely Coupled Systems." *Administrative Science Quarterly* 21(1): 1–9.

Wilson, Ian H. July 1974. "Socio-Political Forecasting: A New Dimension to Strategic Planning." *Michigan Business Review*: 15–25.

Yuchtman, E., and Seashore, S. 1967. "A System Resource Approach to Organizational Effectiveness." *American Sociological Review* 32: 891–903.

INDEX

Guidelines
    content, 50
    outcomes, 51
    process, 50–51
    preplanning, 49

H

Hampshire College, 95
Harvard University, 58
Hershey Co., 18
Higher Education Bibliographic Handbook, 70
Hiram College, 60
Historical perspective, 40, 91–93
Hitt, John, 33
Home economics departments, 15–19, 98

I

IBM, 58
Illinois: public institutions, 26
Industrial/business partnerships, 18–19, 47
Influence of Sea Power on History, 92
Information
    dissemination, 49, 50
    following purpose, 82–84
    guidance and control, 84
    individuals as storehouses, 72
    operational, 83–84
    organizational purpose, 79–80
    sources, 70–71
    strategic triangle for, 81
    systems, 85
    technically oriented, 80
    visual knowledge, 86
Institutional factors (see also Mission)
    competition, 11, 36
    culture, 50
    inward-looking, 62
    loose coupling/diversification, 63–64
    market, 59
    program/clientele/service area, 51
Intelligence as information, 84
International Trade Center, IA, 15
Involvement
    CEO, 50
    faculty, 13, 14, 31, 33–34
    staff, 50, 61–62

revision, 39
statement, 30, 51

Models
bureaucratic, 96
collegial, 96
commitment to status quo, 25–26
contextual planning process, 37, 96
coordinated anarchy, 95
cross-campus departmental review, 33
environmental scanning, 71–72, 77
formal-rational, 94
issues approach, 40, 44–46
organizational behavior, 96–99
organizational development, 95
organized anarchy, 96
Peterson's planning models, 93–96
philosophical synthesis, 95
pictures, 46–47
political, 96
political advocacy, 95
program review, 15–16, 33–34
rational, 96–97
slow paced, 30
STEP/SOS, 72–76
strategic business units, 16
strategic framework, 28–30
strategy formulation, 4–6, 8
straw, 40, 43–45
Strength + Opportunities, 13, 46
structured, 34–37
technocratic/synthesis, 95
two-level strategy, 23

Monte Carlo technique, 69, 70
Morey, Ann, 46
Motorola, 61

N

Nabisco Cookies, 18
National Hospice Organization, 18
Nestle Co., 18–19
Nielson, Tom, 48

O

O'Toole, Peter, 69
Objectives, 13
Ohio Athletic Conference, 60

V

Value changes, 74
Vincent, Richard, 64
Vision
> development of, 21–22
> future focus, 39, 98
> leadership connection, 7, 28

Visualizing, 47, 86–88

W

Walla Walla prison, 63, 64
Washington: economic development, 41
Washington State University, 41, 44
Williams, Harold, 7
Wilson, Ian, 72, 74, 75, 76

X

Xerox Corp., 58

Z

Zi, Sun, 92

ASHE-ERIC HIGHER EDUCATION REPORTS

Since 1983, the Association for the Study of Higher Education (ASHE) and the ERIC Clearinghouse on Higher Education at the George Washington University have cosponsored the ASHE-ERIC Higher Education Report series. The 1988 series is the seventeenth overall, with the American Association for Higher Education having served as cosponsor before 1983.

Each monograph is the definitive analysis of a tough higher education problem, based on thorough research of pertinent literature and institutional experiences. After topics are identified by a national survey, noted practitioners and scholars write the reports, with experts reviewing each manuscript before publication.

Eight monographs (10 monographs before 1985) in the ASHE-ERIC Higher Education Report series are published each year, available individually or by subscription. Subscription to eight issues is $60 regular; $50 for members of AERA, AAHE, and AIR; $40 for members of ASHE (add $10.00 for postage outside the United States).

Prices for single copies, including 4th class postage and handling, are $15.00 regular and $12.00 for members of AERA, AAHE, AIR, and ASHE ($10.00 regular and $7.50 for members for 1985 to 1987 reports, $7.50 regular and $6.00 for members for 1983 and 1984 reports, $6.50 regular and $5.00 for members for reports published before 1983). If faster postage is desired for U.S. and Canadian orders, add $1.00 for each publication ordered; overseas, add $5.00. For VISA and MasterCard payments, include card number, expiration date, and signature. Orders under $25 must be prepaid. Bulk discounts are available on orders of 15 or more reports (not applicable to subscriptions). Order from the Publications Department, ASHE-ERIC Higher Education Reports, The George Washington University, One Dupont Circle, Suite 630, Washington, D.C. 20036-1183, or phone us at 202/296-2597. Write for a publications list of all the Higher Education Reports available.

1988 ASHE-ERIC Higher Education Reports

1. The Invisible Tapestry: Culture in American Colleges and Universities
   George D. Kuh and Elizabeth J. Whitt

1987 ASHE-ERIC Higher Education Reports

1. Incentive Early Retirement Programs for Faculty: Innovative Responses to a Changing Environment
   Jay L. Chronister and Thomas R. Kepple, Jr.

2. Working Effectively with Trustees: Building Cooperative Campus Leadership
   Barbara E. Taylor

3. Formal Recognition of Employer-Sponsored Instruction: Conflict and Collegiality in Postsecondary Education
   Nancy S. Nash and Elizabeth M. Hawthorne

4. Learning Styles: Implications for Improving Educational Practices
   Charles S. Claxton and Patricia H. Murrell

5. Higher Education Leadership: Enhancing Skills through Professional Development Programs
   Sharon A. McDade

6. Higher Education and the Public Trust: Improving Stature in Colleges and

Universities
Richard L. Alfred and Julie Weissman

7. College Student Outcomes Assessment: A Talent Development Perspective
Maryann Jacobi, Alexander Astin, and Frank Ayala, Jr.

8. Opportunity from Strength: Strategic Planning Clarified with Case Examples
Robert G. Cope

1986 ASHE-ERIC Higher Education Reports

1. Post-tenure Faculty Evaluation: Threat or Opportunity?
Christine M. Licata

2. Blue Ribbon Commissions and Higher Education: Changing Academe from the Outside
Janet R. Johnson and Lawrence R. Marcus

3. Responsive Professional Education: Balancing Outcomes and Opportunities
Joan S. Stark, Malcolm A. Lowther, and Bonnie M.K. Hagerty

4. Increasing Students' Learning: A Faculty Guide to Reducing Stress among Students
Neal A. Whitman, David C. Spendlove, and Claire H. Clark

5. Student Financial Aid and Women: Equity Dilemma?
Mary Moran

6. The Master's Degree: Tradition, Diversity, Innovation
Judith S. Glazer

7. The College, the Constitution, and the Consumer Student: Implications for Policy and Practice
Robert M. Hendrickson and Annette Gibbs

8. Selecting College and University Personnel: The Quest and the Questions
Richard A. Kaplowitz

1985 ASHE-ERIC Higher Education Reports

1. Flexibility in Academic Staffing: Effective Policies and Practices
Kenneth P. Mortimer, Marque Bagshaw, and Andrew T. Masland

2. Associations in Action: The Washington, D.C., Higher Education Community
Harland G. Bloland

3. And on the Seventh Day: Faculty Consulting and Supplemental Income
Carol M. Boyer and Darrell R. Lewis

4. Faculty Research Performance: Lessons from the Sciences and Social Sciences
John W. Creswell

5. Academic Program Reviews: Institutional Approaches, Expectations, and Controversies
Clifton F. Conrad and Richard F. Wilson

6. Students in Urban Settings: Achieving the Baccalaureate Degree
Richard C. Richardson, Jr., and Louis W. Bender

7. Serving More Than Students: A Critical Need for College Student Personnel Services
   Peter H. Garland

8. Faculty Participation in Decision Making: Necessity or Luxury?
   Carol E. Floyd

1984 ASHE-ERIC Higher Education Reports

1. Adult Learning: State Policies and Institutional Practices
   K. Patricia Cross and Anne-Marie McCartan

2. Student Stress: Effects and Solutions
   Neal A. Whitman, David C. Spendlove, and Claire H. Clark

3. Part-time Faculty: Higher Education at a Crossroads
   Judith M. Gappa

4. Sex Discrimination Law in Higher Education: The Lessons of the Past Decade
   J. Ralph Lindgren, Patti T. Ota, Perry A. Zirkel, and Nan Van Gieson

5. Faculty Freedoms and Institutional Accountability: Interactions and Conflicts
   Steven G. Olswang and Barbara A. Lee

6. The High-Technology Connection: Academic/Industrial Cooperation for Economic Growth
   Lynn G. Johnson

7. Employee Educational Programs: Implications for Industry and Higher Education
   Suzanne W. Morse

8. Academic Libraries: The Changing Knowledge Centers of Colleges and Universities
   Barbara B. Moran

9. Futures Research and the Strategic Planning Process: Implications for Higher Education
   James L. Morrison, William L. Renfro, and Wayne I. Boucher

10. Faculty Workload: Research, Theory, and Interpretation
    Harold E. Yuker

1983 ASHE-ERIC Higher Education Reports

1. The Path to Excellence: Quality Assurance in Higher Education
   Laurence R. Marcus, Anita O. Leone, and Edward D. Goldberg

2. Faculty Recruitment, Retention, and Fair Employment: Obligations and Opportunities
   John S. Waggaman

3. Meeting the Challenges: Developing Faculty Careers*
   Michael C.T. Brookes and Katherine L. German

4. Raising Academic Standards: A Guide to Learning Improvement
   Ruth Talbott Keimig

*Out-of-print. Available through EDRS.

*Out-of-print. Available through EDRS.

Dear Educator,

I welcome the ASHE-ERIC monograph series. The series is a service to those who need brief but dependable analyses of key issues in higher education.

(Rev.) Theodore M. Hesburgh, C.S.C.
President Emeritus, University of Notre Dame

Order Form

Quantity   Amount

_____ Please enter my subscription to the 1988 ASHE-ERIC
Higher Education Reports at $60.00, 25% off the cover
price.   _____

_____ Please enter my subscription to the 1988 ASHE-ERIC _____
Higher Education Reports at $60.00.

_____ Outside U.S., add $7.50 for postage per series.   _____

Individual reports are available at the following prices:

1988 and forward, $15.00   1983 and 1984, $7.50 each.
1985 to 1987 $10.00 each.   1982 and back, $6.50 each.

Please send me the following reports:

_____ Report No. ___ (_____)   _____
_____ Report No. ___ (_____)   _____
_____ Report No. ___ (_____)   _____

SUBTOTAL: _____
Optional U.P.S. Shipping ($1.00 per book) _____
TOTAL AMOUNT DUE: _____

NOTE: All prices subject to change.

Name _____

Title _____

Institution _____

Address _____

_____

City _____ State _____ ZIP _____

Phone _____

Signature _____
☐ Check enclosed, payable to ASHE.   ☐ Purchase order attached.
☐ Please charge my credit card:
                 ☐ VISA   ☐ MasterCard (check one)

Expiration date _____

ASHE   **ERIC**

Send to: ASHE-ERIC Higher Education Reports
The George Washington University
One Dupont Circle, Suite 630, Dept. G4
Washington, D.C. 20036-1183